LETTER TO THE PREDATOR

(BASED ON TRUE EVENTS)

ELIZABETH ALLRED

CPS INVESTIGATOR

Fulton Books
Meadville, PA

Published by Fulton Books 2024

ISBN 979-8-89427-042-5 (paperback)
ISBN 979-8-89427-043-2 (digital)

Printed in the United States of America

To Pete—thank you for the encouragement and support through every step we have taken together. This book exists because you gave me the faith to believe something good could come from the chaos I call childhood.

To my children—you are the only reason I even want to try.

To my parents—thank you for not being perfect and pointing me in the direction to try and create a better outcome for my own littles.

To the children I work with—when I see you, I believe there is still good in the world.

And to God—thanks for giving me another chance. I won't let you down.

If you continue to hide under a rock and pretend that
child abuse is a problem everywhere else but here,
you will eventually hit your head on that rock.

INTRODUCTION

IT WAS 3:30 A.M. MY brain would not stop its thinking processes. The circular argument of supported versus unsupported, evidence and fact versus opinion and bias continued to scream its awareness into my desire for sleep. I had not had a full undisturbed eight hours of sleep in twenty years. Well, not without double digits of melatonin milligrams. I do my best thinking when my thinking doesn't stop.

After grabbing my phone and allowing the blue light to reawaken my eyes from what my brain was already fighting against, I jotted down this little number. I immediately felt resolved. After thirty minutes of finger fighting the small keyboard on my phone, the result was the warning I wanted. No...I *needed* every predator to know. I was coming, and I was coming for them. And if I couldn't sleep, they should not think they could either.

THE LETTER

I KNOW WHO YOU ARE.

I know what you do.

I know your secrets.

While you believe in the destruction of innocence, I am building their empire of strength. While you hide behind a screen of lies and deception, I am illuminating your identity for the world to see. Your crimes against children are known, and your king has been checked.

Your false sense of power is nothing against knowledge. I am educating the masses. Your reign over the timid has been diminished to insignificance and humiliation.

Where once you felt powerful, I will show you how powerless you really are. I will destroy your safe hold and send in the troops of silent power. I am the drumbeat you quietly hear steadily sounding the alarm of your location.

Where once you thought you were invincible, I will force you to see how weak you really are as I push to uphold all charges against you. Your plea for penitence will only fall on deaf ears.

I am the hallelujah to the tears you have forced. I am the band-aid to the bleeding. I am the kiss upon the scraped knee. I am the arms that lift up the weak.

I will publicly embarrass you. I will ensure your humiliation. I will stand on the wall of justice as a witness against you. I will scream your crimes as a beacon for the silent. I will hold the broken bird in my hand as we destroy your nest of filth.

I am the greatest CPS investigator. I am the strongest advocate to the detective. I am the best witness for the prosecution. I am the clearest law to the judge. I am the smallest and dirtiest cell you will find yourself in. You have no white flag. Your time is up.

I am your infestation, your infection, and your flu.

I am every red light when you are in a hurry.

I am the sign above your door to hell. You will abandon all hope when you hear my name.

I am the water in your sinking ship. You will have none to drink as you shrink from exposure.

I am the acid in your leaking battery.

I am the calm before the storm.

I am the millstone around your neck.

I am the passion of justice.

I am the unpaid interest to your debt.

I am the raven to your Nevermore.

I am the eagle to your liver.

I am Elizabeth.

CHAPTER 1

IN MY BEGINNING… ACTUALLY, I hate it when stories start out like that. There's only *one* "in the beginning" story, and it does not belong to me.

In the state of Utah, it is a misdemeanor to abuse a child. Specifically, Utah code 76-5-109(2-3) states, "(2) An actor commits child abuse if the actor: (a) inflicts upon a child physical injury; or (b) having the care or custody of such child, causes or permits another to inflict physical injury upon a child. (3)(a) A violation of Subsection (2) is a class A misdemeanor if done intentionally or knowingly. (b) A violation of Subsection (2) is a class B misdemeanor if done recklessly. (c) A violation of Subsection (2) is a class C misdemeanor if done with criminal negligence."

It is a felony to abuse an animal. Specifically, Utah state code 76-9-301 (6) states, "(6) A person is guilty of a third-degree felony if the person intentionally or knowingly tortures a companion animal."

I have seen that most people who are pedophiles in the state of Utah see little to no time behind bars. The criminal justice system in Utah is very soft on child predators. This is seen over and over in the media as a perpetrator who has been convicted of abusing a child stands before a judge, whines and cries about what a great person they were, and that they just made a bad choice. Usually, the criminal has pled the charges of abuse down so far that the person is only put on probation and maybe has to pay a fine.

I can only speak to the laws of Utah, but I have heard from several of my FBI friends that travel throughout the nation that this is a problem throughout America.

Still, with all that being said, Mr. and Mrs. predator, you are hereby ordered to stay away from the children of Utah. You are hereby commanded to just stay away. You are not welcome here, and you are not invited to harm our children!

There are many great protectors of children in this state who continue to fight every day to protect the vulnerable. Their efforts do not go unnoticed. And while those of us that carry personal baggage along through our interactions with children that have been victimized, we continue to push forward and demand justice for our clients. We understand there are things that are beyond our control in this great work. But that does not mean we will stop the fight. And at this point, I am bringing the fight to you. You have been warned.

Pedophiles and child predators are being given grace through the judicial system with little accountability for their actions. The crimes they commit against children are forced to live a life sentence in the prison of their minds. The victims are actually the ones that are forced to be sentenced to a life of unbearable pain while the perpetrator is given forgiveness by a quiet judicial justice system. The system that created agencies to investigate and fight child abuse have silenced the victims with the pathetic whimpering of the abuser.

This passion of mine to become a child abuse investigator started out of desperation for a job that I could provide for my family. Since 2003, I have worked with the youth in the state of Utah and advocated for their voices to be heard. As a child abuse investigator, I have witnessed firsthand that there are bad people who do bad things to the "littles" of the great state I work for, and I investigate those allegations.

Like an eye doctor (I don't know of any that don't wear glasses), people tend to get into fields of employment that they know and have a passion about.

I know abuse. I know neglect. I have made a personal vow to be the voice and the fight for the children I serve.

Hell doesn't last forever. Especially if you are not supposed to be there. Working in the field of child abuse investigations, unfortunately, has made it seem that hell is an all-encompassing world that has no limits to the amount of abuse it will inflict upon the most vulnerable. Abuse does not care what your gender is, your age, your learning ability or disability, your income level, or your background. Abuse doesn't care where you are from, what religion you are, or what your last name is. Abuse doesn't care if you are homeless or live in a mansion. It does not discriminate and accepts all forms of deprivation to a healthy society. Abuse has one goal, and that is to create an uneven playing field between one in control and one that is vulnerable. Nothing is equal with abuse, and nothing is fair. Abuse never has, and never will, make sense.

Yet, for some reason, the most valuable assets we have as a society (our young and innocent generation) are often tossed to the side and forgotten in hopes that if the abuse is ignored long enough, it will just go away.

Despite task forces being created, victims' rights groups acknowledged, and political campaigns pounding pulpits in anger, little is done that really makes a difference in the actual world of child abuse. I cannot tell you how many cases I have investigated where the child made a disclosure of the abuse, the perpetrator admitted to law enforcement the crimes, and the charges filed only to be pled down and the perpetrator being let off with a slap on the wrist.

I have seen children die. I have seen children so badly abused they are now in permanent states of paralysis. I have seen caseworkers quit and attorneys resign because a perpetrator was getting probation.

The state of Utah is now becoming a hotspot for pedophiles. Out-of-state predators are seeking out the children in Utah to abuse because, and I have heard this with my own ears, if they get caught, the courts are so lenient to child abusers, they will only get a minimal sentence, if sentenced at all.

So why do I do this work if the system is set up to just let the bad guys go? Because it can change. It *has* to change. The change has to start somewhere, and I believe it starts with this very conversation.

I was diagnosed with failure to thrive at a very young age. This would be my introduction to my life of trials, whether self-inflicted or familial. With the diagnosis, I was hospitalized in the Tripler hospital in Honolulu, Hawaii, where both of my parents were stationed with the navy. It is well-known among the locals as the "pink" hospital.

At the time of my young diagnosis, my dad was on a submarine somewhere in the deep blue depths of the Pacific Ocean. My mom was alone and depressed with me, her new baby. I made her a mom, something she always wanted to be, but postpartum became her undiagnosed diagnosis, if you will.

All her support systems were physically and emotionally unavailable themselves. After a few weeks in the neonatal intensive care unit, I was released by a caring and concerned nursing staff to a mother who had been thoroughly educated in the importance of positive interactions with me, her first child and brand-new baby. They clearly instructed my mother it was inappropriate to leave me for hours at a time, crying alone in my crib. They encouraged her to look past the obvious and unspoken postpartum to ensure I had regular feedings, diaper changes, and social interactions. The nurses drew the parallel between my current state of care (neglect, to be specific) and the potential negative effect the neglect would have on my emotional and developmental well-being. They gave no speech on self-care or postpartum blues because, to be cliché, back then, you did not talk about such things.

Little did I know that the very diagnosis of failure to thrive on the beginnings of my human experience would predict the life battle I still face today. I have found that today, this diagnosis has manifested itself into the unfortunate diagnosis of depression and anxiety. I continue to struggle with the uncertainty of the love and care anyone has, or could have, for me despite the proof my life continues to exhibit. A good friend of mine called this the "imposter syndrome" and "rejection sensitivity."

This realistic war raging inside of me tells me I will never amount to anything more than that little baby annoyingly crying in the background. However, this is not a story of a crying baby. This is a story of a strong woman, rocking the baby inside her and actively comforting the sorrow within. Then, as my story goes on, I put the sleeping baby to bed to tend to the toddlers tearing up my house. I play with those toddlers. I let my soul be childlike and sensitive because there is work to be done. And at some point, that little crying baby inside of me wakes up and needs attention, and I have to be able to take care of her.

When we each think of our own individual story, and we *all* have a story, we must consider the very way the story is told. This is our narrative. How we tell our story matters.

Facts stay facts, but the mind interprets those facts a certain way, which then becomes perspective. Facts don't care about feelings. But perspective is what makes us fragile and vulnerable. Perspective transitions into emotion that interferes with fact and causes an action. Actions become the "how," as in how we act in a given situation.

We can change the "how." We can change our perspective. We can align our perspective to that of God's, and in doing so, our actions are aligned with His perspective. We will begin to see ourselves as He sees us. We begin to tell our story as He would tell it.

Some cultures call this perspective a third eye. (Heads up to all you Third Eye Blind music fans. There is a deep meaning in that name.) We do not want to be blind in our third eye. Having that third eye is considered a state of enlightenment, an ability to see spiritually what we cannot see physically.

In the Church of Jesus Christ of Latter-Day Saints, we call this the Holy Ghost. The perspective of the Holy Ghost is that of our Father in heaven. He tells us the truth and where to find it. He guides our hearts and minds to understanding what we cannot comprehend because of the pain and abuse our physical lives have suffered. When adhered to, the perspective of the Holy Ghost is lifesaving. I mean that literally and eternally.

When we consider the beautiful story of Jesus healing the blind man, do we consider the perspective of the blind man? He was poor, persecuted, a beggar that only annoyed those passing by. But when engaged with the Master himself, his physical eyes met Jesus, who would soon atone for his sins (on which the Pharisee's blamed the man's parents for his blindness), but his narrative, the blind man's perspective, saw the Son of the very God standing in front of him with compassion and purpose.

My story (and to be clear, my perspective) is one that considers the positive per my situation, no matter the difficulty of the subject. I have a firm belief that people can change as I have been able to put myself back on the path to my God. I have also witnessed my parents as they pushed through their own demons and trials. I held (and to some degree, still do) resentment and disbelief at some of the choices my parents made that unfortunately added to the self-worth wart I have on my soul.

While still in Hawaii, my dad returned to shore in the USS Abraham Lincoln and discovered his new baby daughter (that's me, in case you missed it) had been admitted to the hospital. His response to my trauma was to move us to the mainland in Idaho Falls, Idaho, where he began working for General Electric as a nuclear engineer. Depression set in on my mom even more so than before. My dad found her lack of mothering skills offensive and, instead of being supportive to her mental health crisis, ran from it by self-medication in the form of liquid antidepressants known as "Keystone." Budweiser was saved for when his buddies came over to party with him.

It was at these gatherings that at the age of two, I sipped my first beer left within my reach from a coffee table covered in overflowing ashtrays and half empty beer cans. I was too young to appreciate the impact this first sip would have on my indifference toward alcoholic beverages. The environment of acceptance of this substance would one day weaken my ability to find other methods of appropriate use of dealing with life's challenges.

The fact that my parents were obviously indifferent to a curious toddler easily impacted by opposing religious values, and lifestyle choices made little difference to bringing more children into the world. I was two years old to the day when my little sister was born. We will call her Sister 1.

And not too long after that (approximately two months), my mom announced her intention to kill herself. Still living in Idaho, my mom locked herself into the bathroom with a bottle of some serious medications and razors. The sheer emotional terror I felt listening to the screaming between my dad and mom still haunts me. By the time my dad was able to talk my mom into unlocking the door, everyone was so exhausted that we retired to bed and never spoke of it again. My parents thought the best solution was to try and have another child to bring joy into my mom's life, and my little brother Michael was born in 1981.

Of course, this led to further bouts of depressive behavior and inappropriate coping skills from my mom. She would sleep all day, leave her very young children unattended, not do the dishes for days at a time, and inappropriately yell and scream at her children who were exploring the world.

When I was five years old, I had been playing in our backyard with something I was probably not supposed to be playing with. I wish I could remember what that was, but the psychological impact of the consequence has shaped that memory to only include the punishment. My mom grabbed me and beat me with a belt until I was unconscious. I woke up from the attack to her rubbing medicine on my back while uttering incoherent apologies. I believe the situation also proved traumatic for her as there was never another child beaten with a belt by her hand to the same degree of results.

My dad continued to do exceptionally well at work and was seen as a work horse to his leadership. A better job opportunity was presented to him, so my parents sold the Idaho house, and we landed in Midland, Michigan, where two more of my siblings were born (Sister 2 and Brother 2) within a few years. This brought the family total to five young children with two adult "children" (children meaning my mom and dad) attempting to parent them.

By the time I was old enough to attend school, I found myself walking a couple of blocks home, rain or shine. Eventually, a neighbor complained at the sight of a tiny six-year-old red-headed girl walking alone, and my mom signed me up to ride the bus. My stop was three blocks from my house. One sunny afternoon, I was walking home with a boy from my class. His house was directly on the corner by the bus stop. He was the nicest kid in my class and I, not being aware of the gender stereotype of "cooties," considered him my best friend. We sat on the bus together that day, walked to the next block over, and then he turned back to walk to his own home.

However, on this one fall day, his older brothers and uncle called from my little friend's house to come back and "play" with all them. At the time, the two blocks I had left to walk seemed an inconvenient distance for me to walk. I also did not want to go home as doing so would just mean seeing my mom sleeping on the couch with the house a disaster, small babies dirty and hungry, and my role of caring for everyone for the night would begin. I looked back at my friend's house and thought of all the fun that might actually be had.

There was no fun and no "play" to be had. I walked in the dark living room and stood motionless with my hands on my backpack straps. The door slowly closed behind me, and then the chain locked from above, too high for my six-year-old frame to reach. I turned to look for my friend, who had been by now locked in his room. I noticed the door to his bedroom had a similar chain lock as the front door, but on the outside, ensuring he could not escape. I could hear him crying from behind the door, which changed my emotional emergency response from playful to fearful.

I was held against my will for hours. Terrible things happened to me in that home. I can still smell the cigarette smoke that deeply penetrated into the couch cushion in which my face had been forced into as the boys took turns sodomizing me with foreign objects and their body parts. When I would kick and scream, one of the boys picked me up like a sack of potatoes and carried me over to the stove, where they held my bare feet over the burner until I stopped screaming. I was then returned to the couch while their black-filled eyes threatened my cooperation as they took turns violating my innocence.

It was not until they heard the sound of my friend's mother pull up in the gravel driveway of the trailer house that I was dressed, threatened with silence, and pushed outside into the cold Michigan air. My innocence was gone like the smashed-out light of the embers on a discarded cigarette.

It was dark and cold outside. I wanted to run home, but each step shot new pain up from my groin, to my thighs, and up to my abdomen. The cold wind only felt colder as the unfamiliar red wetness dripped down my legs into my shoes.

As I walked in the front door, I saw my mom sound asleep on the couch, in front of the blaring television. My brother Michael was in his playpen with a poopy diaper sagging almost to his knees. I tried to wake up my mom and explain with words I did not know, or have, the horrors of having just been sexually and physically assaulted. I was barely able to speak. Tears could not even come as I was still unclear as to what had just happened.

Trauma was the new language of my young understanding. I tried and tried to gain her attention, but the story could not tell itself. And I didn't even know how to speak the language of this foreign experience. My mom hardly rolled over to open her eyes and look at me.

Knowing I was not going to be able to get her attention to the degree I knew I needed, I procured the strength a child that young should not have to muster and took a shower the best way that a six-year-old could. I watched all the signs of abuse wash down the drain. My mom never asked, recognized, or questioned the marks or bruises that had been forcibly put upon my body.

For months, I was subjected to verbal and psychological abuses while riding the bus home. I would beg my mom to drive me to school or pick me up, and there was always a denial. The bus driver finally questioned me about the daily tears I cried. As I shared with the bus driver my fear of the older boys without the details of the sexual abuse experienced at my friend's house, I was hand delivered by bus directly in front of my home for the rest of the year.

My mom refused to acknowledge my emotional retreat, and instead intensified her emotional distance from me. I think back now as an adult and a mother myself and wonder if this reaction from my own mother was more understandable than she intended. A survivor of abuse herself, she was struggling with mental health issues that her own situation was so debilitating and kept her frozen in depression.

Eight years old seems pretty young to try and kill yourself, but that was my age when I experienced my first suicide attempt. I put a bag over my head while lying in bed and just prayed for the Lord to take me. I just wanted to die. Of course I did not die! I removed the bag myself and continued to cry hysterically for a sense of peace and comfort. I felt alone in a crowded, loud, and chaotic house.

Our house was too small for our growing family. My dad continued to work late hours to remove himself from the home as much as possible. His bosses enjoyed the productive outcomes my dad produced for them. And as such, he received another promotion, which came with another job transfer, this time to Illinois.

Caring for my younger siblings became the expectation. This started to become the norm of daily living, and my mom now had the expectation that I would parent my siblings. My resentment would continue to grow.

Later in life, I learned the importance of the word *no*. No is a complete sentence. It has such a significant impact on our need for boundaries. God uses it with us, and we should also learn how to apply its powerful application in our relationships with others. Using the power of the word *no* will help us be assertive. We can stop justifying others taking advantage of our ignorance or unwillingness to face potential conflict by simply saying "no." By giving yourself permission to say no, you stop giving away what you don't have.

The fact is, a lot of our anxiety and disappointment stems from the expectations we place on others. When they fail, it resonates to us as our own personal failure. Only God is allowed to have expectations. He is allowed to have expectations because He is perfect. We should not set others up for failure, and that includes emotional impact. We are not caring or watching over ourselves if we allow the failures of others to impact our personal well-being. By setting up expectations in others, we are trying to fix and control everyone else without taking responsibility for our own part of the problem.

Resentment toward my mother stemmed from the inconsistency in my mother's parenting. She was either angry and yelling for the whole neighborhood to hear, or she was depressed and not mentally or emotionally in tune to the needs of her young children. She continued to sleep on the living room couch all day and was blissfully ignorant to the insidious chaos surrounding her. All or nothing.

The same can be said for my dad. He was either lecturing us, spanking us with a drilled-out plastic paint stick, putting us in a chair to learn to sit still for four hours at a time, or locked in his office alone from anyone or anything that might require his affection or personal time. All or nothing.

Because the chaos of the home meant little structure, there was not much that could be said to our personal hygiene. I had not been taught the importance of dental care, clean and fitted clothing, or simple hairstyling techniques. My hair was red and frizzy. My hair was never in style or attractive in my opinion. I did not look like everyone else, and as a child of eight, I wanted nothing more than to blend into my surroundings. But without the knowledge as to how to make that happen, I was an easy target for bullying and few friendships.

I was jealous of Sister 2's hair. She had gorgeous, long, dark hair. I was unblessed with red, curly, frizzy, and unmanageable hair. Given the lack of personal hygiene my own mother perfected, it was left to me to learn how to tame the beast on my head and take personal interest in cleanliness. I would not discover how to really do this until I was a teenager, and that came through the wisdom and help of *Glamour Magazine*.

And because I was only a child caring for other children, there was no consistency to my parenting. The job of parenting, supervision, and general hygiene fell on the shoulders of the two people who had emotionally passed the torch to an eight-year-old. We grew up mostly unkempt, unbathed, unfed, and unattached to parental figures.

My mom eventually got a job at a local greenhouse to get out of the house. Slowly, she moved from being just a warm body to finding some sense of self-worth and responsibility.

At the age of eight, there was also a profound shift in my family culture that became obvious to my parentified brain. My father's parents were active and diligent members of the Church of Jesus Christ of Latter-Day Saints. At the age of eight, I was ripe for baptism, which meant my grandparents were hounding their oldest son to be a better father figure and get his manhood in check. My parents sat our growing family down and announced our trip by plane to Salt Lake City, Utah, where my parents would be sealed in the temple.

We stayed at my grandparent's home while in Salt Lake. I'd never been in such a clean and organized house. The feeling there was sweet and calm. My sheets were clean; I was so used to sleeping in the pee-infused sheets from younger, not quite potty-trained siblings squeezing into bed with me at night that the smell of fresh linen was tantalizing. I felt like little orphan Annie entering Daddy Warbucks's mansion for the first time.

Of course, the limited parenting skills of my mother and father did not change overnight. With the overwhelming pressure from her mother-in-law to perform at perfect levels, my mom never felt she was good enough for my grandma.

Despite the fact that my grandmother was nothing but kind and gentle in all her words of wisdom, her expectations of at least being "less harsh" in mothering bounced off my mom into thin air. On the porch of my grandparent's home, the day before we went to the temple, Sister 1 refused to hold still while my mom was brushing her hair, and my mom, with all the strength she could muster, I witnessed my mom spank her butt so hard that Sister 1 lost her breath for a good five seconds. I stood in shock, believing that this parenting style had been left back in Illinois, and the newly "sealed" family was going to be better. I watched in horror and embarrassment as Sister 1 peed her pants from crying so hard.

My grandma rushed out to the porch to save Sister 1 while I stood in shame and utter embarrassment at my mom's actions. My grandma attempted to scoop Sister 1 up in her maternal arms and wipe her tears but was cut short by my grandpa's intervention. He pulled my grandma into the house. I could hear him pleading with her to stay out of it, and that my dad would take care of the situation when he got back.

He never took care of the situation.

The next day was busy with travel from being taken from one location to another, left with this uncle or that cousin at different times, and being pulled by the hair by my mom on a regular basis.

On a day that was supposed to be special, it was not what I had hoped for and ended just as bad as it had started.

After his service in the navy, my dad maintained several friendships he had developed along the way. One such friend was also a member of the Church Of Jesus Christ of Latter-Day Saints. He was from Idaho and drove down to Utah to go through the temple with my family.

After the events of the temple, we went to visit them at the hotel this friend, and his family were staying at for some much-needed pool time. I did not know how to swim, but the idea of jumping into the pool water seemed utterly exciting! One of my dad's friend's daughters, we will call her Amanda, was close to my age and had embraced me as her new best friend. I watched her carefully jump in the deep-end over and over as I dipped my toe little by little on the tile-pool edge. I looked at my parents, visiting and laughing at the other side of the pool. My mom was constantly shoving my half-asleep Brother 2 off her lap to go swim with the rest of the kids. It was around 9:00 p.m., and he was just a baby. He was a little tired, to say the least, and I continued to watch him plead with my mom to let him crawl in her lap and sleep. His attempts were fruitless, and her irritation continued to grow.

My knowledge that I did not know how to swim was put to rest by my new best friend, Amanda, who encouraged me to just move my arms in the water and I would be fine. I took one last glance at my parents, hoping they would offer some guidance or rules about being by the deep end (especially if you can't swim), but not one glance was issued in my direction; not one thought was given about where I was.

Amanda beckoned me from depths of the unknown, and I smiled and leapt. My head never surfaced, and my arms didn't move under the water like my friend's did. I started to panic and found myself sinking faster and faster, no matter how hard or fast I moved my arms like Amanda showed me. Then just as fast as I went down, I felt the straps of my swimsuit being yanked up as I was pulled to the side of the pool by another unknown older girl.

All I can remember about her was her deep blonde hair waving like a mermaid off her shoulders as she helped me back to the pool tile my toes were so familiar with.

By the time I caught my breath and realized what had just happened, I was infuriated at my parents once more. Yet again, I found myself alone, fighting for my life, and my parents a world away, with not a care for my existence to be found. I ran over to the adult-gathering spot where Brother 2 had abandoned his quest for my mother's lap and was laying on the cement, sound asleep. I yelled at both my parents, telling them of my engagement with death, and asked them why they weren't watching me and why they didn't save me. I was crying and still trying to catch my breath.

My mom's response, "Well, unfortunately you didn't drown, so what's the big deal?"

Amanda stayed quietly in the background, and as the hurtful words left my mom's mouth, my new friend's mother stood up and left the pool, taking Amanda's hand while muttering something under her breath about parenting and mothers, and that she could not stand to be around "her" anymore and had enough…and… and…and…and Amanda was gone.

Returning to Illinois, the lack of routine and parental care only took months to reassert itself. My dad started sneaking his old reliable coping skills of cigarettes and beer for a year until he was confronted by my mom. Being outed by his drunken speech and the smell of nicotine on his person came more as a relief for my father rather than cause him to return to better health habits. He embraced being back in the saddle with full-fledged alcoholism and chain-smoking.

My mom returned to her normal harsh parenting habits on display when others were watching, and neglect ruled the day when no one was looking. She sought employment at a greenhouse to help her get out of the house for a few hours during the day. But her job at the greenhouse ended as quickly as it began. I guess there is this unwritten rule about showing up to work, and when you do show up, show up on time, not two hours late, or you will be fired.

My dad started taking business trips for weeks at a time. This was not to anyone's benefit. The minute he left, so did my mom. I still don't know where she would go for days at a time. She would make me promise not to tell my dad she had left us alone. Until one night, no amount of lies or disappearance could be ignored anymore.

After my mom would leave for the night, I would gather the sleeping little kids into my parent's bedroom. I would lay them all on the king-size waterbed and sleep at the foot of the bed like a watchdog waiting for the owner to return. And that is exactly how it felt: we were nothing but animals, treated like dogs, not children.

Around 1:00 a.m., as I cuddled next to my little brother Mike, I was awakened by the shattering of a glass window in the room next to my parents that was designated as my dad's office. I laid there in scared, shocked, and in terror as the unfamiliar manly voices whispered words I could not make out. I quickly covered all of us in a huge blanket. No one on the bed had moved, thank goodness, so I knew the little kids were still asleep. I laid down and pretended to be asleep, watching the waves in the bed become smaller and smaller. I held my breath, hoping the bed would stop moving completely.

I could hear them breaking the glass on my dad's gun case. I knew they were going to come in here and shoot us. Where was my mom? Why did she leave us? I knew something bad was going to happen, and here it was! This was how I was going to die. Maybe she told these guys to come kill us because she was always saying she wished I was dead and how much she hated us. It seemed like the men were in the house for hours when, in fact, it was only minutes. Because my dad would always lock the office with a padlock on the outside and he was the only one with the key, they were not able to get into the rest of the house. They tried a couple of times to get the door to open, but soon, their attempts stopped, and they left the same way they came in, out the broken window.

I laid awake for hours watching the little kids' chests move up and down in a slow, rhythmic motion, hoping they would stay undisturbed by the break-in. I was *not* getting out of the bed, and I did not dare move in case they came back through another window. I laid in my own urine for hours; getting up to go to the bathroom might trigger the bed to move. A sound, a light, anything to draw attention to my brothers and sisters was to be avoided. I couldn't cry, and I had no one to call. 911 was not a thing I had been educated to yet.

When my mom showed up around 6:00 a.m., she staggered into her room to see a pile of problems laying on her bed. She asked me what I was doing awake, and I pointed to dad's office. I couldn't even talk. I was still so scared. Even in the presence of my mother, I experienced no relief from the terror of that night. I knew she wasn't going to protect us in any way. She wasn't able to get into the office because of the padlock; it was meant for her as well as us small children. She quickly ran outside to examine the broken window to my dad's office. She called him frantically, the broken and obvious lie entangled in the details of the event, none of which came close to what actually happened. My dad caught the first flight home.

The police showed up and took inventory of the stolen guns and items. My mom was quick to remind me that I must tell my dad she was home all night and did not leave the house, but I had no intention of covering up for the woman who had left us to die by the intruders. I threw her under the bus as quickly as she had left us alone.

No one asked me any questions about the situation. I was told by my dad to stay away from the investigation and, by my mom, to keep my mouth shut. So I did. My brothers and sisters and I were not shot. We didn't die. No one tried to kill us. At least that night, the bad guys didn't. We always knew it was the druggie neighbors that stole the guns, but it would take too much effort on the Braidwood Police Department to do an investigation on people they already didn't care about. That night just became one more reason for me to harbor the growing resentment toward my mom. I dug my heels in deeper for the appreciation I had developed for guarded behavior. I was resolved to never let my guard down. No one was ever going to protect me, and the night we were robbed proved my mom didn't care for my survival.

The burglary did lead to a few household changes. I am not sure if it was for the better, but they were changed nonetheless. My dad made my mom promise she would *never* leave us alone again, no matter what.

Because she was still determined to not parent, my mom found the cheapest solution to her problem. She hired a babysitter! Sweet! Welcome to the family, babysitter Donna. I should probably mention the following:

1. Donna was an older woman (much older) who had spent years in prison for physically abusing her children.
2. Her children were removed from her custody because of the abuse, and she never saw them again.
3. She was on parole when my mom met her.

Apparently, that meant she met all the qualifications of a good babysitter, so my mom deemed it appropriate to hire her.

First day on the job… Let's see. I came home from school to find this strange and very witchy-looking woman in our house. She was cleaning. What was she doing in our house, and why was she cleaning? No one has ever done that, not even the people who live here. She smiled at me as I stood there, not moving. If eyebrows could talk, the furrows would tell the story of skepticism and doubt. Mike, Sister 2, and Brother 2 had been bathed, but from the look on their tear-stained, swollen eyes, it did not look like it had gone well. They were sitting as still as statues on what appeared to be a couch. I had forgotten we even had a couch as the piles of laundry usually found their way to the large horizontal surface. We also had carpet I had not seen in years. Usually piled with garbage and dirty diapers, the floor seemed like a welcoming place. I was certain I was in the twilight zone. And to top it all off, my great grandmother's crocheted blanket hung neatly off the back of the couch behind Sister 2 and Mike, and they did not dare move. Something was wrong. Sister 2 was a toddler, and she never sat still. Mike was always exploring, and his panicked look said, "save me," as I met his gaze. Where was my mom?

I asked the witchy woman who she was, and she introduced herself as "Donna."

"Where is my mom?"

She quickly replied with the most obvious response, "She is not here."

"Where is she?"

"Children should not ask so many questions. It's rude."

"But I need to know where my mom is and when she will be back!"

With that, I was met with a painful reminder of her previous statement that children should not ask questions. The burn on my cheek told me everything I needed to know about this woman, and because I pride myself on being a quick learner, I never asked her another question.

Knowing Donna was going to be our new caretaker quickly changed the pace of freedom in my home. I knew how to survive. Her new rules and ungoverned discipline proved to be painful and abusive to say the least. I watched daily after school Sister 2 and Mike received beating after beating with the closest hard object available in this woman's reach. Mike would have bruises all over his back and bottom. Sister 2 would have her hair long dark pulled and bruises on her face from being slapped.

No one knew the rules that they were breaking, just the moment they were broken because of the marks left on us. We were clean. We were fed. But we were once again left to our own devices of self-preservation. We were told not to say anything to our parents because we were naughty children, and children should not talk. We *did try* to beg our parents into listening to what was happening with Donna's abuse, but there was no aid. My mom's usual response to me was to listen and be respectful. If I did not break the rules, I would not be in trouble. And then, when I would watch the transition of my mom leaving and Donna arriving, I would hear my mom give explicit permission for her to spank us if we needed it.

I guess Donna's idea of spanking and mine were totally different. I had been beaten by both my mom, and now Donna, to the point of unconsciousness. Mike had so many marks on him, he was starting to look like a purple oompa-loompa. But it was not until Sister 1 received the ultimate smack down of us all that authorities had to intervene.

Sister 1 and I would ride the bus home from school every day. On one particularly memorable bus ride home, one of the kids had a cute little stamp. With the tiny lid removed and a little push onto a surface, it left an imprint of a purple pumpkin. We all took turns taking the stamp and applying small smiling pumpkins to our hands and arms with the colorful stain. It was fun and new.

Upon arrival home, Sister 1 and I raced to the front door. Sister 1 was the stupid one that went into the house first. I stood still on the front porch, holding the screen door open behind her. Frozen in place like a deer catching the snap of grass under the predator's feet, we were greeted by the wicked witch, Donna. Sister 1 foolishly held her coat in one arm, exposing the elementary school tattoo artistry of happy purple pumpkins overlapping one another in a linear fashion as she made direct eye contact with Donna. Donna immediately saw the stamp marks inked on her skin and grabbed her tiny arm. The witch's long almond-shaped nails pierced into Sister 1's skin so hard that blood started to come from the pointed cuts. Donna dragged Sister 1 into the house before she could even drop her backpack. I saw Donna grab the stick used to realign our delinquent ways and raise it high above her head. Sister 1 had no time to retreat or escape the death grip of Donna. The stick landed on Sister 1—her butt, her arms, her legs, her torso—in such frantic motion as I had never before seen. Donna was furious.

Apparently, Sister 1 broke the rule we did not know about, of never putting anything on your skin! *Ever*! Doing so was a devilish act, and because we were devilish children, as I heard Donna scream into the air, Sister 1 had to be taught that such acts of tattooing (or in this case, putting a child's smiling purple, purple stamp anywhere on your body) were "of the devil."

I knew the hits must have been physically exhausting for Donna as she had to take a break every so often to catch her breath. I remember seeing blood coming from Sister 1's mouth and nose after she stopped crying. I had never seen a human body turn swollen and purple so fast in my life.

I knew there was nothing I could do to save Sister 1, so I allowed the screen door to slam back to its shut position and turned around to run as far away from Donna as I could. I left Sister 1 to take the beating for the both of us. I was not going to let that woman touch me! I thought Sister 1 was dead the moment I saw her eyes pause open and her screams of pain stop. I did not want to die. I had never seen another person get hit so hard and so many times in so many different places. I had seen and experienced enough already, and I knew the wrath Donna had released upon Sister 1 was going to kill me too.

I ran out of the house and hid in a tree until my dad got home. My mom was still nowhere to be seen or heard from. No one even knew where she went. I waited for my dad to go in the house to see what I thought would be Sister 1's dead body, and when Donna left, I made a mad dash inside.

As I quietly walked through the front door, I saw Sister 1 laying on the couch with my grandma's black and flowered-crocheted-patterned blanket comforting her lower body. Her eyes were swollen shut. Her arm had a cloth carefully wrapped around where Donna had viciously scrubbed off the first layer of skin from the elbow to the wrist. I wonder if this experience is why Sister 1 does not have any tattoos to this day… Hmmm… Guess she learned her lesson that ink is of the devil.

Sidenote, I wonder what Donna would think of my tattoo today. As I look down the length of the inside of my left arm that read, "I am enough," I bet the notion that at the age of forty, I braved the tattoo world and inked my arm with the reminder that predator's like Donna never win. I bet that would upset her. (Insert fulfilling smile here!) Guess I should have had the devil beat out of me too.

Anyway, my dad did not ask me anything about Sister 1's obviously upsetting physical condition until he was confronted by authorities. Donna had told my dad Sister 1 fell, and no questions were asked. Until…

Sister 1 and I went to school the next day. I am assuming a kind and caring teacher saw the physical state Sister 1 was in and called the authorities because when we made it home that day, Donna was not there. We were greeted by my smiling mother and some social service workers. My shock actually came because my dad was also home. This was really confusing to me and, to be quite honest, scared me.

My mom pulled her false caring excuses out from everywhere she could to appease the social service worker. She pleaded innocence, that had she known about Donna's extreme discipline styles, she never would have left her children with such a monster. Then, in unbelief, my mom pulled me in close to her and pretended to hug me. I was so set aback by the lies in my mom's story but chose to go along with it.

Even though it was all lies, my mom was holding me close in a loving and caring way. She acted as though she loved and cared about me. It felt so nice, even for a false moment, and even though I knew it was a cheap attempt at parenting, she was, in that moment, kind and protective.

Of course, it all ended as soon as Social Services left the house. But it was nice while it lasted.

My dad pulled me into his makeshift office later that night. He asked me why Donna beat the crap out of Sister 1, and I did not say anything about what really happened. I explained we were playing with a stamp on the bus, and it made Donna mad. That was the language I knew. I did not know it was a crime, and her attempt to kill Sister 1 left me very confused.

Apparently, according to my dad's explanation to me, it was my fault Sister 1 was beaten. I was supposed to be watching out for my siblings. Because I allowed Sister 1 to stamp her hand (this unknown "no-no", Donna lying to my dad because she almost killed Sister 1 in her attempt to "discipline," and then my family being reported to authorities) had become the focal point for my parents losing the only babysitter they could bribe to watch us. Yes, somehow, it was my fault.

Apparently, we children were so unruly and undisciplined.

Apparently, I had allowed Sister 1 to make the cardinal sin of taking a stamp and marking her skin.

So apparently, the fault landed on me.

I received a spanking that night from my dad as my apparent punishment. Like everything else in my life, it was painful and memorable. My dad grabbed his homemade spanking stick by its six-inch handle and spanked me a dozen or so times on the naked tush with the two-inch wide and half-inch thick yellow plastic stick he had drilled holes into, which allowed for a faster swing and more force on impact.

To this day, I don't understand the logic behind any of the discipline that went on in that house. I will, however, be forever shamed at the fact that I left my sister to almost die at the hands of a witch.

With Donna gone, my mom had to actually stay home and watch us, or at least pretend to do so. There was one particular Saturday I remember. My dad was gone on a work trip, and my mom had been missing for hours. I went outside to play with the neighbor kids in their greenhouse. We were not supposed to play in it. It was forbidden mainly because of the illegal marijuana plants they had growing in there, but hey, it was a fun place to play.

Hours of happiness and joy went by. It was a really fun Saturday, only to be disrupted by my mom racing out of the house, screaming my name in a manner known to all as the "you are in trouble" name. This particular tone of voice was the one I was most familiar with. It usually came before something would come flying out of nowhere and painfully hit me somewhere on my body.

I peeked my head out of the forbidden greenhouse to see my mom rushing at me like an angry bull seeing red in a Spanish fight. I was no matador, but the plastic spatula (not my dad's spanking stick thank goodness), frantically swinging it in a fit of rage above her head made me hesitate to leave the sanctuary of the marijuana plants.

Now I may have been young, but I was not stupid. Or so I thought. The chase began and ended quickly. Unfortunately for me, trying to run in an effort to escape the swinging cooking spatula only made my mom even more upset. That scene was the precursor to intolerable pain headed my way. As per the usual, I had no idea why I was being beaten and furiously dragged by the shirt collar back to the house, being swatted at with the now-broken spatula on various reachable parts of my body.

I kept asking my mom between my sobs what I had done as she dragged me back onto our property. As she let go of my shirt, I fell to the ground and covered my butt with my hands as she swung the spatula up one last time. My mom stopped in midswing as we both paused to see an ambulance driving up our half mile driveway. My mom turned back to me and pointed the spatula in my face and then to the ambulance, all while yelling something of it being my fault Mike, Sister 2, and Brother 2 had almost died, and I was supposed to be watching them.

I was smacked across the face with the plastic spatula. My hand met my cheek in a shock of disbelief and confusion. My mom picked me up off the ground by my shirt collar again, this time causing it to rip and pulled me into the house. I was pushed into a now-crowded bathroom and observed my three youngest siblings lying on the bathroom floor, being forced to vomit into the tub.

I had gathered the crime scene evidence with my limited comprehension of events and concluded Mike, Sister 2, and Brother 2 had consumed an entire bottle of Flintstone vitamins because they were hungry and had been looking for something to eat, which was, once again, per the usual in house. I watched as my mom forced her finger so aggressively down my brother Mike's throat in an effort to get him to continue to throw up.

The medics had entered the house at this point, and I was told to go to my room and await my reckoning. I stepped into the hall to get out of the way and watched as Mike, Sister 2, and Brother 2 were hauled out to the ambulance. I thought they were dead, or at least going to die. I started to cry.

When the ambulance left, my mom continued to yell at me that I was a bad and irresponsible sister. I concluded that she must be right. It *was* my fault as my mom continued to tell me. I concluded they were going to die. I walked back to my room with the feelings of defeat and hid out until everyone returned from the hospital. For almost killing all four of my siblings by this point, I was feeling pretty bad and guilty in a very confused way. Thank goodness my mom only grounded me for a month for not parenting, cooking, feeding, cleaning, storing medications away from small children. I don't know how I got so lucky on that one! (I'm being sarcastic for anyone that can't read sarcasm.)

Jump ahead several years, and now eight total children. That's right, my genius parents had eight kids. They could not get along, and every night ended the same way: my dad drunk in his locked office trying to avoid all human contact with anyone that had the same last name as him.

We had moved into a home large enough for our family. It was a blue two-story modular home. Unfortunately, the bigger home was not only to accommodate the growing number of children but to create a physical boundary between my dad, my mom, and their paternal responsibilities. The drive to compete for affection and attention from my parents dwindled as I slowly learned that such attempts were futile.

The only consistency to my life was the chaos. Each day ended the same way. My dad would become instantly agitated at the sight of the messy house, the noise of screaming children, the smell of a baby's poopy diaper, and the touch of tiny hands clawing and pawing at him to be held. Agitation would turn to anxiety and then yelling. Someone would eventually be spanked and pushed to the side. Everyone was told, "Stop! Leave me alone for five minutes! Let me get through the door!"

By 7:00 p.m., after my parent's nightly screaming match occurred behind their shut bedroom door, my dad would emerge with a hung head and slouched shoulders. Sometimes, if I were lucky, I could catch him sneaking down the stairs. I would try to throw some little tidbit of knowledge I learned at school at him in hopes of starting up a conversation. My dad's response was most often a one liner, usually some comment insinuating my childishness and stupidity. I would be left in his shadow, standing alone as he continued down the stairs to the dungeon I longed to be in with him.

No one was ever hugged or asked how their day was. We were left to our own devices, mostly raising ourselves. No one helped with homework, reminded us to turn in assignments, quizzed our spelling, or guided our childhood upbringing. No one even told us to brush our teeth or to put pajamas on, for that matter. We all had the understanding that our parents were not to be disturbed; doing so would lead to serious emotional and physical consequences.

If we were so lucky to have interactions with my dad, it was in the public arena. One particular occasion is still brought up at family gatherings as its impact was quite resounding. It was at one of the summer office parties for my dad's work. We were at Kankakee Park and playing with some of my dad's coworker's children. I caught, out of the corner of my eye, my dad laughing and talking with other adults. I felt so happy inside to see him so relaxed and at ease with other people. As a child, I remember feeling proud of my dad. I wanted to know what it was that these people were doing to get that smile on my dad's face. I had to know the trick. I approached the conversation and silently stood in the background, listening intently for cues on words to use so I could join in on the fun. As I continued to listen in, I heard my dad enthusiastically recall a story from his past. He was an excellent storyteller and had everyone laughing and enthralled with his experience. As the story continued, I remember that I had never heard such excitement in him before. People were commenting and laughing, so I jumped at the chance to join in. I asked one question. It was as though the tires of the moment could be heard screeching to a halt. My dad grabbed my arm and swung me out of the conversation. I was handed off to my mom, and she instructed me to go play chicken in the road, citing that a few less of us around might not be such a bad thing.

Eventually, when being a father of eight children and a husband to a manic-depressive wife was too much, he bailed. I do need to say that even before he left, the smell of a missing father was still strong in our home.

At the age of fourteen, my mom decided a road trip across the country by herself with eight small children would be a good idea. We traveled in a red maxi van that we nicknamed the "Bloodmobile" because someone was always getting injured in it or by it. Several rest stops along 1-80, my mother unsuccessfully attempted to let one of the little kids go with a trucker, only to be stopped by my belligerent attitude and instinctive protective mode I developed at a young age.

As we were driving through Nebraska on our way back to Illinois, the most incredible police stop happened. One minute everything appeared to be fine, and the next minute my mom was being pulled over at gunpoint in the middle of the hot freeway. Apparently, we had been on a high-speed chase and did not even know it. All eight of my brothers and sisters and I were left on the side of the freeway while SWAT, drug dogs, and helicopters buzzed overhead searching our red maxi van. After what seemed like hours of sitting on the side of the highway, staring at the endless fields of grain, sweating and burning in the hot Nebraska sun, and doing all I could to entertain my siblings to prevent them from running onto the highway, the officer explained to my mom she was not allowed to drive through the rest of the state and that I had to. I didn't even have a learners permit!

My mom had been driving drowsy and swerving all over the road. She had been followed for miles without realizing the cop was behind her. When the police officer asked how fast she thought she was going, her smart response was, "I don't know! The speedometer doesn't go above 80 mph." As we packed everyone back into the van, I could see the officers laughing off to the side about the massive piles of dirty diapers, old food, and clothes their well-trained drug dogs had sniffed out, all remnants of our two-week vacation in the van. I often wondered what ever happened to that officer's reputation.

When we returned to Illinois, my mom attempted to kill herself again. This time, she was admitted into a mental health facility in hopes of conquering her own demons.

My dad returned to the house with his parents. They stayed three weeks. It was one of the most impactful times I can remember as a young teenager. Our home was cleaned up. We were cleaned up. The alcohol disappeared. The happiness that had been missing for so long began to peek its tiny head above gray clouds looming over our home.

My grandma was putting the little kids to bed, and I could hear her reading them a bedtime story. I was read to for the first time, though unintentionally. I sat in the hall out of sight, around the corner of the bedroom door, and just listened. I never knew how wonderful the sound of a matriarch's voice could be until I heard it being used to soothe small children to sleep.

I can remember it all vividly. There was a beautiful bronze bust of Jesus Christ that my grandparents had given to my parents sitting peacefully on a bookshelf. As my grandmother read, and several other times throughout my chaotic childhood, I found myself staring at the face of Christ in this statue form, feeling calm. I knew in that moment that anything good, calm, peaceful, or pleasant would only come from Him. I also learned in that moment, listening to my grandmother's voice and looking at that statue of Christ, that despite all the trauma and chaos, the Savior could be found, even in the midst of hurt.

I also was introduced to the beauty of prayer. My grandparents gathered all of us together each night in our living room for something I learned to look forward to. Sometimes, my grandpa would pray. Sometimes, my grandma would pray. But whoever prayed always said something I had never heard before. They prayed for each of us by name. I loved hearing my name in a prayer and the pleadings my grandparents put before God on my behalf.

With my mom out of the home at the mental hospital, my excitement about life started to begin. There was structure and love. I felt validated, and I was allowed to be a kid. Being a kid, however, was difficult for me to embrace, and I actually was very uncomfortable with the allowance. Despite normalcy being introduced into our home, the shift in parental presence challenged me.

My mom was eventually released from the hospital and returned home. Upon her return, she thought she was stronger and healthier than she actually was, but the results had a more devastating impact than anyone anticipated. My dad left with my grandparents, and all my sense of family with them.

My mom's depression worsened, and it took her out of the home on a consistently inconsistent basis. Chaos ensued in every corner of the house. I would be left to care for my seven younger brothers and sisters while she disappeared for weeks at a time.

Several times, she attempted to enforce boundaries and rules with not just me, but herself. I had been parentified at such a young age that the idea of her taking back that role intensified my resentment. On one hand, she tried to regroup her parenting style but would relapse and fall into even deeper pits of depression. As she tried and tried to show consistency in discipline, my efforts to prove she was a fraud increased. My parenting skills at fourteen years old were amateur to say the least, and the shift of power was being felt by everyone in the household.

Police officers became regular visitors whether through well child checks by the Division of Child and Family Services or neighbor referrals for loud obnoxious behavior. The total number of officer visits that summer was over seventy. Random and dangerous people would come and go. Transients and squatters began taking over our house. When my mom would return home from whatever it was she did or had been, we would have battles, physical and verbal, about my desires for her to step up and be a mom. And like all parent-child battles, I would never win.

She finally talked the local hospital into admitting me into a psych ward. She exclaimed to the orderly that she feared I was suicidal and wanted me out of the house. She said she did not want the other kids to be influenced by me. She told the doctors my dad was a cross dresser and that he hated me. Her explanation of my mental state to admissions was enough to have me in a secure locked down mental institute for a week. I was roommates with a seventeen-year-old who had sliced every inch of visible skin with a man's disposable razor. She would talk to me in great detail about cutting and pain and scars. This knowledge would come in handy at a later point in my life. But she would scream in the middle of the night, oftentimes waking the entire floor. I would listen to her pick at her flesh for hours as I prayed I would be able to leave this horror house.

On one Sunday afternoon, I had an unexpected visitor. The nurse came into the doorway and asked me if I would like to visit with my dad. As the tears rushed like a river down my face, my dad met me in the doorway. I spent a week at the hospital before my dad came to visit me. He had me immediately released and returned home. That memory ends there with disappointment and unnecessary secondary trauma I had just endured for no clinical reason.

The next two years continued in absolute chaos with my mom in and out physically and emotionally. My dad had moved into an apartment in the local area but that was still too close for his comfort. He never came to visit, even though he was within a five-mile distance. I called every day and asked if I could live with him, and the answer was always the same quick response, "No." We were never allowed sleepovers. Once a month, we were allowed to visit my dad for a couple of hours on a Saturday at his discretion. When the agony and repeated pleas from his children were too much to handle, he jumped from state to California, claiming it was a mandatory job transfer. I will always believe it was because being in the same state as his ex-wife required too much effort and emotional responsibility. It was just too much for him. And just as fast as he moved out, he moved on.

At the age of sixteen, I had had enough. Parenting feral children with the resentment I held was taking its toll emotionally and physically. I was at the end of my sophomore year in high school and had endured the most I could take from local bullies who constantly teased me and my siblings. I was in fights in bathrooms with girls saying mean things to me. I was in fights with kids on the bus saying mean things to my siblings. I was in fights at home with my siblings for annoying me.

I did not feel safe walking down the halls of the school because of the comments said to me, about me, or about my family. The tactics used to intimidate me were becoming more and more severe. Comments about my physical appearance, my puberty changes, my lack of knowledge about sex in general were plastered in permanent marker on my locker. Notes were passed to me with threats. These were the days before social media bullying created cyber trails so evidence of such intimidation fell on deaf ears and he or she said status. No adult ever took my side. I was just a "price kid" after all.

My dad was gone, and I got my driver's license by the grace of God and a desire only a tornado could blow away. My mom was dating anyone who had a checkbook. One guy's credit card after another guy's check came and left.

Sister 1 had become my biggest enemy as I watched her start taking on the attributes of my mother.

I joined any after school club and sporting team that would take me just to get an extra couple of hours out of the house. I justified the cost of the bullying as worth its price just to escape my home life.

Sister 1 and I would fight and argue like two cats or pit bulls in a ring. It was never one-sided, and our disdain for each other created warring alliances within the sibling group. I took care of my brothers and bonded strongly with them. Sisters 2 and 3 teamed up against us, and it became one group of four against another group of four. Something small would trigger me, and hateful speech would be spoken from my mouth. I was a brat. I was mean. I was never physically abusive to anyone. Physical altercations, yes. Physical abuse, no. But be assured there were plenty of good ol' Seven Brides for Seven Brothers fights (but without the song and dance).

Eventually, my internal wars of self-worth and esteem would catch up with my childish survival skills, and I would have to make the most crucial crossroads decision a young girl should never have to make. Do I stay and save my brothers and sisters from this inevitable chaos of disastrous lifestyle choices being perpetrated upon us by our parents? Or do I save myself?

CHAPTER 2

IN 2003, I GRADUATED FROM Utah State University with a bachelor's degree in sociology. For me, it was an easy degree to obtain and felt like there were a lot of options for me in seeking a career. Ideally, I wanted to pursue a legal degree, but that fell by the wayside as I now found myself with two small children under the age of two and a soon to be ex-husband.

My husband at the time had been expelled from college for cheating on papers, and the role of breadwinner quickly fell onto my lap. I took my prized possession of a degree and started to look for jobs that required my self-proclaimed expertise.

After weeks of searching, a job posting caught my attention with the state of Utah's Division of Child and Family Services (DCFS) team. My heart exploded into my soul as I knew this job would become my career.

I submitted my application and waited for a call for an interview. Nothing.

I waited two, three, four weeks. Nothing.

And then, upon the idea that I was overqualified based on my life experiences and about to give up, I received a call from a lady requesting my presence for an interview. The state of Utah was doing a mass hiring for DCFS, and they wanted to know if I would be interested in interviewing for a position.

Yes, yes, and yes!

The next week, I put myself together in the most professional look I could conjure together and arrived at my first official job interview. I walked up to a sliding glass window that had a young woman sitting in a swivel office chair. As I approached, she slid the glass to her left, and I introduced myself as "Elizabeth." No more Beth. I wanted the rest of my professional career to be new and full. I did not want to short myself one opportunity, and that even meant my name. I explained I was there for an interview with DCFS. The woman smiled and handed me a clipboard with a piece of paper. She asked me to fill out the questions the best I could, and that there would be no right or wrong answers. She then pointed me back to the waiting room to sit in a stained green-and-red fabric chair with faux oak armrests.

The waiting room was littered with old books and toys that had lived a life prior to showing up in this causality of a calm space. Once in this room, the books and toys found had a little left to give and created a false diversion for the parents and children waiting to meet or visit someone behind the locked down and secure door in the adjacent rooms. Once in a while, I would observe what appeared to be a caseworker open that locked down and secure door and call a name. A child would usually pop up from the filthy stained carpeted floor and run to the caseworker with opened arms. The caseworker would take the child back while the other adults in the room would ignore the chaos and continue reading the two-year-old "Parents" magazines with ripped off and blacked-out names and addresses of the rightful owner and donor of said magazines.

I looked down at the questions. One: What would I bring to DCFS that would help improve the lives of others. I wrote down that I had a deep understanding and appreciation for child safety and was willing to learn how to improve the lives of others in Utah. It was a genuine answer and heartfelt without all the deep baggage associated with my own life experiences. Three more questions like that, and I finished the essay questionnaire.

I walked back up to the lady at the window and knocked at the glass as she was obviously sidetracked with a conversation going on behind her. She approached the glass and pulled it back again to the left. I explained I had finished the essays. She instructed me to keep the paper and take it back with me when I was called for the interview.

I patiently waited thirty minutes to be called back. It was interesting to observe the chaotic comings and goings of the DCFS space. I observed all the people and children and wondered that each of their stories was that led them to be involved with the agency. Were they a victim? A perpetrator? A parent? A foster parent? So many questions!

And then, "Elizabeth?"

The locked-down, secure door opened, and a large tall man half stepped through the frame, peering around the room for someone to respond to the name. It sounded so formal to have my name said in such a way that required me to be on top of my game.

The man introduced himself as Dave, one of the supervisors in the office. Dave appeared to be wearing a red plaid shirt that he had worn every Thursday for the last twenty years. The fabric on the collar was worn so thin it had turned white and curled up underneath itself. His khaki pants held onto a story Dave's thinner days and showed signs of several meals eaten in a hurry while driving and then attempts to be washed clean. Dave did not appear to have cared what he was wearing, but more about what he was saying. And I was listening.

I stood up and smiled at the man. Shoulders back. Chin up. Hand out. Solid shake.

I handed him my clipboard of essay questions to which he quickly glanced over and said, "Okay, let's go."

I followed him into his office, where I observed another larger man named Steve sitting at a small circle table with three chairs cramped around it. Steve did not try to hide his obvious uncomfortable position in his metal chair that was too small for his large frame. He did not stand up as I entered the room but motioned to the empty chair next to him. I did not take offense to Steve's choice to remain seated upon my entry. I was not here for pleasantries.

A few warm-up conversations between Steve, Dave, and me, and the interview questions soon began. Dave looked over my essay questions and handed the clipboard to Steve.

"Well, they messed up the questions again," Dave said.

I sat confused as I was not sure if it was something I did wrong, if I just blew an interview, or if I had to retake a test.

"Do you mind if we just ask you some questions about how you would handle certain cases?" Steve asked as he kept his eyes glued to my essay responses.

"Sure. Throw it at me!" I said with confidence.

And the first bombshell hit.

Dave opened up my mind to the world in child abuse in one question. The answer would be the one that landed me start to child abuse investigations.

"You get a case involving a six-year-old child and sexual abuse. Older brother is seventeen and is the alleged perpetrator. Older brother makes the six-year-old give him blow jobs right before he has anal sex with her. When the six-year-old refuses, he grabs her head and forces her mouth on his penis to the point that he suffocates her, and she passes out. What would you do first?"

My mind paused. My body paused. My breathing paused. My blinking froze. While this question is not meant for the soft of heart, it was meant to point out the realities of the world in which DCFS works. The shock factor was an important part of my interview.

I rolled my shoulders back and knew the next thing that came out of my mouth would make or break my future. I knew part of the questions asked were to weed out the weak and tenderhearted, those not made for this line of work. But that was not me. I knew these were real stories, real children, and real experiences. The shock factor of this question was important, and I understood why Dave just went for it. But would I bite? What would I do first?

I furrowed the elevens between my eyes as I pondered, *Who else knows and needs to know? Where are the parents and what are their responses to their son's actions? Is the child still in the home? S*hould *the child still be in the home if the parents are not willing to mitigate safety?*

I communicated my answer to Dave's question with more questions to gain more clarity on the situation. Dave and Steve both sat up in their silver metal, state-issued chairs and leaned in to my willingness to have a conversation about where to begin.

Forty-five minutes later, Dave had to cut the interview off and shook my hand in closure. As he walked me back to the solid locked doors that led to the freedoms of the world and free space my mind would never have again, he told me it was the best interview he had ever had with a potential employee. We shook hands one last time, and I left the DCFS office with a job and career path to my passion.

I was officially a DCFS caseworker!

It is unfortunate that the caseworkers hired today are not given the same shocking questions. The division today does not provide a three-month training to its employees and has skimped on a lot of the education and training provided. Caseworkers today are not even close to being prepared for the caseloads they are given on day 1. They are not prepared for the level of abuse we are seeing today and the turnover rate in caseworkers is evident of that fact.

This is a hard job, and everyone coming to this field knows that. But when you see a two-year-old child for the first time with a boot imprint on his back that matches mom's boyfriend, you get a real sense that you are in the foxhole now. There is no going back.

And when you have to listen to the detailed events of a three-day rape from an eleven-year-old's point of view, you cannot unhear those things. So why so soft? This is what I want to know from the caseworkers today? The work has not gotten easier. If anything, it's *way* worse. So why is the state not doing a better job of training these caseworkers for the realities of child abuse today? My tiny bit of advice goes straight to these caseworkers… You got this! You are not alone. You have one hell of a job in front of you, and these children are depending on you to keep them safe. Don't be afraid of using your own voice, even if it shakes. You have a world of hurt you are going to have to swallow, but it will be the best tasting meal you ever had! I've been where you are, and there is a happy ending.

My first few months of working for the state of Utah as a DCFS caseworker were all about the training and indoctrination into policy and procedure. The training was a piece of cake for me. Each day, the group of new hires that I belonged to gathered together in a room and waited for the session to start.

I was always early, with pen and paper in hand, for extensive note-taking. Each day, one of the trainers began our sessions with words of caution, that what we were about to see and hear would be repulsive and horrific. We were given recommendations for self-care and encouraged to speak to our superiors if we mentally felt like we could not handle the secondary trauma about to be heaped upon us.

I was not sure what I was about to get into, but as each training session ended, I wondered if the scary stuff was ever going to come. I had already lived the life of a so-called victim. While my new coworkers were taking breaks every thirty minutes or so to regain their composure, I was shrugging my shoulders like the details of each case could not faze me. I had already lived that life. Nothing was shaking me, and the stories were less than terrifying.

I was uncomfortably comfortable in the world of child abuse. I wanted to save the children and had an obvious ability to separate myself from the abuse to peel apart the thick skins of each case. I found myself quite good at my job. It was starting to become easy for me to conquer each case and be the voice for children. My supervisors gave me high praise, my name ran up the chains of command as a quick learner and sure-headed employee. My name became well-known throughout the DCFS community. Seasoned workers asked my opinion on cases and sought my advice for case proceedings. My passion for saving children got me out of bed every day, to drive an hour and a half to work and then back home for the next year.

And the better I got at my job, the worse my marriage became.

When I started to stand up for myself, my ex would fight back even harder. When I wouldn't do something the way he wanted it done, verbal and physical assaults would ensue. When his pornography addiction came to light, his excuses and blaming became louder. When he started to take his anger out on my children, I decided enough was enough.

My ex had put my children in the tub one night before bed. I heard my son crying a short time later in the bathroom. I quickly walked to the bathroom door to see what was going on and proceeded to see my ex poking my son extremely hard in the chest with his index finger. He was yelling at my son to listen. I instinctively grabbed my son away from his dad and asked what he thought he was doing hurting a baby like that. I attempted to take my son into the bedroom to stop the assault. His dad immediately grabbed him from my arms. I was no physical match for a tug-of-war challenge and decided to play it safe and let him take my son back from me. He took my son into the bedroom and dressed him for bed. As my daughter was still in the tub, I decided it was best to get her out and ready for bed.

When my ex left the kids' shared room, I pulled up my son's pajama shirt to reveal an already-forming bruise in the middle of his chest. I pulled my son's shirt back down, kissed his cheek goodnight, and decided it was time for the ultimate confrontation in parenting appropriateness. This would be the last time I would allow my husband to hurt us.

My ex had gone into the living room to watch TV. I stepped between the TV's glaring light and his view of whatever hunting show he was watching. With fear in my voice, I started out the conversation in a very directive and factual manner. His discipline was less than appropriate and he was never to poke my son again.

My ex's follow-up comment was meant for me to back off and allow his behavior as I had in times past. He stated it was completely appropriate to poke children as hard as you can in the chest because his dad did it to him. He stated it was a well-known joke in their family that their dad had a shorter index finger than normal because he had been disciplined in the same manner.

When I would not allow his excuse for this type of discipline, he became more and more agitated. I knew what was coming and started to bare down for the inevitable. He stood up and started to yell at me for treating him like one of my DCFS clients. He claimed I was the abusive one that made him feel like a terrible parent, and that he acted like he did because I brought that behavior out in him. He started to get in my face and poke me in the chest in the same manner he had just poke my son.

When I would not back down, stood my ground, and refused to let him talk to me or act like this anymore, he pushed me so hard across the room, I tripped and fell to the floor. At the time, we were living in a basement apartment, and the carpeting was covering a cement slab. My head hit so hard on the floor I blacked out for a moment, positive that when I tried to sit up, my head was pounding so hard I knew I had just received a concussion.

My ex left me on the floor and went back to sitting on the couch watching TV. I slowly got up and grabbed the cordless phone. As I walked into the living room with the phone in hand, I told him to leave. He refused. I warned him to leave or I was going to call the police. He refused, this time with a laugh. He was calling my bluff. I dialed 911.

When the police arrived, I was still standing in the living room at the shock of what just happened. My husband was cuffed and taken away in the back of a cop car. I was now the product of an unwanted domestic violence case.

CSI arrived and took pictures of my head wound and my son's bruise on his chest. The police left me several contact numbers for assistance in processing the next chapter of my life, including protective orders and court dates. That night, I slept in my rocking chair with my daughter cradled in my arms, pondering the common thought processes of most people who experience domestic violence. Did I make the right decision or not?

It was about midnight when I was awoken by a knock on the door. My ex-brother-in-law was in my doorway, asking for my ex's wallet. I went to the bedroom to retrieve the wallet, still feeling incoherent and confused. When I returned to the living room, my ex-brother-in-law loudly berated me for my decision to call the police. He was physically bigger than my ex, and the idea of having another encounter like I just experienced hours previously started to rekindle the sense of fear in my soul.

I handed over the wallet and shut the front door. I began again down the emotional road of feeling no man would ever have compassion for my situation and would only take advantage of my emotional insecurities. Why would I have expected it from my ex-brother-in-law? I was not new to this scene, considering how my ex's own father had reacted when he was told the news of my being pregnant with my son and having a remote control thrown at me. Having my ex-husband's brother pick up the verbal pieces where my husband left off came as no shock either.

If you know anything about domestic violence, then you will understand this next self-created chaotic nightmare. If you don't, let me explain. Statistically speaking, a woman will leave a man seven times before she finally leaves him. It will be in death or divorce. I was on number six apparently.

I discovered the little savings I had stowed away had been drained overnight by my ex-brother-in-law for bail money. I had supposed the request for the wallet was for identification purposes but quickly and unfortunately found out too late it was to be for bail.

This was the only money I had and the only bank account associated with my name. It just so happened to be a shared account with the same person I just had put in jail. Now I was financially stuck and obligated to whatever choices were being made in my name, even without my knowledge. My decision to leave was now even weaker, and I was finding it more and more difficult to stay separated.

After months of court hearings and violations of the protective order by both my ex-husband and his family members, I caved and asked the court to dismiss the protective order. I was convinced by everyone that he was going to get better and loved me and the kids. He wanted to make our marriage work and blamed his atrocities on the fact that he was too far away from home. I was the only one working, and the stress and disappointment of not having a job was being used as an excuse that he was too embarrassed, and the strain was too much for him to bear.

He designed a plan for us to move closer to his parents. My ex-mother-in-law had convinced my ex-husband the reason for the domestic violence was because I did not love him enough. My ex then convinced me that I could remedy his feelings by moving with him back to his hometown. Here, he would receive the support he needed to be the husband I needed him to be. In return, my ex promised me that I would benefit from learning to be the kind of wife he needed me to be.

I was so confused by what was happening and had little direction or guidance. I had prayed to get an answer on how to proceed with my marriage but only felt drawn to the idea I did not want to get a divorce. I did not want to have the same kind of marriage my parents had.

Being so ignorant about what marriage really was supposed to be, I knew what it was not supposed to be. I based my decision to move with my ex closer to his parents on the one resolute from my high school years that I did not want to be like my mom.

I had no plans to continue this single-parent lifestyle. I feared that doing so would lead me down the path of destruction I experienced from my own mother's inability to embrace single parenting.

I transferred DCFS work locations to an office closer to my ex-husband's hometown. We only lasted nine more months before I had moved out with my children for the final time.

It was not long after we moved to our new home I had learned that my ex had been having an affair with our daycare provider. The reasoning for even having our children in daycare was curious, but he stated he needed three days a week to look for a job, and putting the kids in daycare was our only option.

I was familiar with the long commutes to and from work so the hour-and-a-half drive every day did not bother me. The extra three hours it gave my ex to be with my daycare provider did, however, bother me.

When I attempted to put a stop to their relationship, I was accused of having the affair, and the table turning began. The physical violence picked up right where it left off. I packed a U-Haul and left town with my favorite people in the world, my kids.

I filed another protective order and awaited the results. I had enrolled my son in preschool in our new town, and my apartment was almost a block away from my office. My ex's attempts to bring our marriage back together stopped. He was now empowered by all his family and community members with financial assistance and moral support to end our marriage and file for the much-needed divorce.

I felt stuck in the middle of a state where I knew no one but the people I had investigated for abuse and soon-to-be ex-relatives that had drawn a line in whatever sand exists. I had no one. People who had once been supportive of my leaving the abusive relationship had dwindled into nonexistence.

I received divorce papers at my work within one week of my leaving. He had been able to somehow afford the most expensive and slanderous lawyer in the area, thanks to the generous donations from his parents.

He was demanding custody. There was no one on my team. I didn't even have a lawyer. He had drained my bank account and refused to try and negotiate any sensible solution in ending our marriage. The pressure was unfathomable, and I had a hard time understanding what my next step in the process needed to be to maintain some sense of propriety. We both knew we were getting divorced, but I had not even had time to look into retaining representation.

Decisions were being made for me at this point, and the loss of control over my life found me falling apart at the seams. I started to make choices I would never have made six months prior. When once I had spent time conversing with God in the temple for peace and understanding, I now abandoned what could bring me the quickest sense of self-indulgence and misery.

I felt alone and abandoned by God and excused my behavior with statements of resentment toward my ex-husband's ability to get away with all the horrible things he had done to me and the kids. He was, in my eyes, getting away with murder.

My behavior spiraled out of control. I started drinking with so-called friends. While these people were probably trying to help get out of my marriage, I failed to see it was for only their sexual gratification and not my moral compass.

My mental health was failing fast. Every time I opened myself to someone, it shot me in the face. My lifestyle choices were turning against me. When I did something right, there was little to no recognition. When I did something wrong, it was shouted from the rooftops with terrible retaliations. I was never going to win in this life, and becoming vulnerable had only hurt me thus far in my existence.

I began to battle with myself spiritually in regards to what I had and knew and what I wanted and did not know. Thus far, the only thing I could chalk up as successful life choices was my mission and two beautiful children. I went back to that mental space over the course of the next several weeks.

My poor lifestyle choices were sinking me fast into despair. Despite thinking initially that I was wanted and cared for, I knew the reality was completely opposite. Drinking just numbed the reality I was living in, and I had to keep coming back to the depression raging in my body. Sleeping around only pushed the spirit I desperately needed away.

Cases became more difficult for me to work, even though the stories were blending together. I was becoming callus and cold to my clients and developed a quick temper and reputation for being "too aggressive" in my approach. I had little compassion for the drug addict parents and desire to buy meth instead of milk.

Environmental neglect cases became my favorite because they were easy for me to work with. I rejected the sexual abuse cases and sent them (if allowed) to other caseworkers to investigate. Physical abuse cases were open and shut as far as I was concerned.

When a child presented with a cigarette burn intentionally left on his genitalia, he would be removed and placed into foster care for adoption. When a child was shaken almost to death, she was removed and placed into foster care for adoption. When a five-year-old was left to care for her three younger siblings because Mom was strung out on the couch, they would all be removed and placed into foster care for adoption. I did not want to work any other way.

I reviewed my survival skills from my youth and realized quickly that the only reason I was able to get through the trauma of my childhood was because I often relied on the relationship I had with God to get me through. I sat at my card table that stood in place of a dining table in my apartment listening to REM's "Everybody Hurts." For some reason, the song that I had never paid any attention to before in my life was shouting at me louder than any person, if they were in the room, could have.

Everybody hurts. I was not alone. I might have been alone, but I was not really alone. I was not better off, or worse off, than any other person. I was in the same group of people who had experienced life and failed as the guy next door.

As a young girl, I never questioned my beliefs because I always held them to be fact. I despised the hypocrisy of my parents' lifestyle choices versus their words of obligation to be faithful in all things. I was eating my own words that "Facts don't care about your feelings."

It actually deepened my resentment toward my mom as she would say one thing and then do another. This fight had led me closer to my religious foundation and wanting a desire to have a relationship with Christ. The closest I felt to the love of my Savior was when I felt so alone and desperate for acceptance from the human race. That bond and relationship of trust was developed so early on in my life, I knew, and still know, I could not deny the reality of God's love for me.

Some believe culture to be an influential factor in what I did next. However, that religious culture was never a part of my life. I was not from Utah. I was actually more rebellious while living in Utah than any other state I had ever lived in. I was not a part of the community, mainly because of my job description and choice to avoid people.

I had no family close to me to help guide me into any choice. The decision to go seek forgiveness from God by talking to my ecclesiastical leaders was one based solely off the love and respect I had for God and God alone. While all men in my life had been a sliver in my finger that I could not heal from, God had always been the healer for me and the only friend, the only true friend, I had ever had. I knew I had to make my relationship with Him right again.

I had battled feeling His abandonment only to discover that sometimes no is an answer. I realized over the course of six very saddened and spiritually unhealthy months that I was asking God to tell me what I wanted to hear. I was not listening to what He was trying to say, which is exactly what I did not want to hear. Who, honestly, likes to be told what they are doing is wrong and then turns to embrace that truth? I believe that for most of us, as humans, it is too difficult, and it takes a person willing to lose everything to change for the better.

This next decision was going to cost me everything I had left, but one I had to make. I picked up the phone and called my current bishop to schedule an appointment.

I was going to make vulnerability look good on me if it was the last thing I ever did.

CHAPTER 3

I SAT ON THE HARD plastic chair, facing three clean-shaven men with the most genuinely distraught facial expressions I had seen in years. Their ties still remained crisp and snug under their necks as the long Sunday continued to turn late afternoon into a late evening.

I had just spent the last few hours in this office answering questions, explaining myself, and justifying the inappropriate actions I felt entitled to participate in over the last six months of my life. I had just left a terrible and abusive marriage and succumbed to the false notion that if my ex was going to make it to the celestial kingdom, I did not want to be there with him!

I knew my justifications for committing such sins were false but continued to break as many commandments as I could without actually breaking any laws of the land. The excuses and behavior sounded good in my head, but when I was speaking each sin out loud, I heard myself clearly see the fool's errand I was on. My back and shoulders slouched in a cowardly form in the chair, hoping the law of mercy would have taken pity on me by simply letting me walk out of the room a "repentant soul."

Deep down I knew there was no appropriate justification for my actions. I knew every sin I committed was a personal choice. I was not justified in my behavior because of the actions of another. I had served a faithful LDS mission and used to teach this stuff! I watched the lives of others change for the better by simply sharing the principles of the gospel. How then could I possibly think I was above these very principles?

I thoughtfully executed my words to the bishopric as I continued to mentally accept whatever was going to come out of this encounter was for the betterment of my soul. But the anxiety over what would eventually come would not leave me.

As I finished my verbal vomiting of unacceptable behavior, I was asked to wait outside while they discussed what to do with me next. I spent thirty minutes in the office hallway by myself, with my thoughts, which is always dangerous. These chairs were a lot more comfortable and softer, covered with cushion and red upholstery. Why couldn't these chairs be in the bishop's office? I began to bounce my knee with my arms folded across my chest. My head would not stop thinking. I leaned forward as though I had just been punched in the gut, in hopes that by some weird scientific method, the racing thoughts would just "fall" out of my brain onto the floor, and I could stomp them out. I contemplated whether to just leave and go home or stay and face the music.

I began mentally yelling at myself for being so forward in making this appointment to begin with. My brain kept fighting with my heart. My soul was the innocent child in the middle of the battle. "Why did you call the bishop and set up this meeting? Are you stupid?" "Why didn't you just keep your mouth shut?" "Yeah, but if I didn't call and get this taken care of, I could never forgive myself for living a lie."

No one would have ever known, no consequence would have ever been given, and no lives would have been ripped apart if I would have just kept my mouth shut. But my only desire in life was to be the mom to my children I did not have growing up. I wanted to be better. I wanted to be honest. I wanted to live up to the standards of truth. I could not have done that with integrity, and I mean *real* integrity, by sitting idly by and watching my soul become an innocent victim to an all-out brain-heart war.

My brain started to win me over as I impulsively tried to devise an escape plan where I would just leave. I kept thinking, *Why in the world am I even here sharing the most intimate details of my life with men I don't even know? Who in her right mind would choose to embarrass herself like this? What am I doing here? Just leave… Just leave. Just get in your car and drive the three blocks back to your empty apartment.*

My two small children were visiting their dad this weekend, and they were supposed to have been dropped off after this meeting. I had started renting an apartment a month ago after leaving my marriage on the third and final attempt. I had finally felt safe enough to escape via an official expedited protective order. With the law on my side, the last straw of abuse was all it took for me to pack up my kids and belongings and drive an hour and a half away from the mess once called "marriage." And yet, despite knowing the kind of man he was, I felt unnecessarily guilty for taking them away from him and allowed supervised visitation on the weekends. This particular weekend would end up being the worst one of my life.

I continued to sit unrested in the hall while people I did not know occasionally passed by. I tried to act like I was not there for discipline purposes. My swollen red eyes, hands full of wadded up tissue, and the quick averted stare gave me away as I tried to play it off as though I was sitting outside the principal's office, waiting for my reward for good behavior. Before I could follow through with my chance to escape the worst moment of my life, I was summoned to return to the bishop's office. Despite what my insides were feeling, I kept my head held high and a smile on my face. My pride was all but gone, and I had no courage left to face their decision. I faked the acceptance of what I knew was coming.

The room was uncomfortable and quiet, except the yelling, screaming, wailing, and crying I was doing silently to myself in my head. The men at the thick hardwood table refused to make eye contact with me. Whether that was through embarrassment or sadness, I will never know. Tears unwillingly leaked from their eyes. The man in the middle of the table, my bishop, was also trying to not cry as obvious by the words that could hardly be understood as he slowly and softly spoke to me. I mentally was checked out, and although I knew what he was saying was true and important, I just could not quiet my thoughts enough to pay attention.

I kept looking left and then right at the men. I looked up at the standard picture of Jesus Christ in the red robe on the wall behind the men. Hammered into the carpeted wall on the left was a picture of the first presidency. On the right was a picture of the Manti Temple. I found my gaze slowly bouncing between the crying men, the pictures on the wall, and my black dress, which was obviously the most appropriate color choice for this moment. I kept thinking about how dead I felt inside. Death would have been sweeter and more welcomed than the next few sentences I really paid attention to.

"Elizabeth," the bishop spoke, redirecting my attention to his face.

He placed his hands on the handbook in front of him and told me again and again how much he knew and felt the Savior's love for me personally. I knew what was coming and kept wishing he would just cut to the chase and spit it out.

"The three of us knelt down in prayer while you were in the hallway and prayed fervently about what to do in this situation. All three of us continued to receive inspiration that we were not to disfellowship you…" There was a long, unnecessary pause, and for a split second, I thought there was no way I was going to get away without a consequence for my actions. They were not going to disfellowship me? Was that even an option? I tilted my head in confusion as the bishop then slowly continued, "We have been directed by the Spirit to excommunicate you."

Everything stopped.

The world finally stopped spinning, and like a movie stuck in slow motion, I could hear or think nothing. I felt nothing. I stared through the three men. I couldn't cry, I couldn't move, and I couldn't breathe. The bishop continued, "We have clearly been told that we were to excommunicate you, or you would be lost to your heavenly Father forever."

Then like someone slapped me back into the present moment, my thoughts rapidly began to drown me.

My head leaned forward, and tears streamed down my face. This…punch in the gut, bouncing knee, thoughts spilling out onto the ground…posture returned.

After months of emotionally falling apart and purposely trying to self-sabotage my eternal salvation, my decisions finally caught up with me, and I sat in the worst possible place of my life: the bishop's office, being excommunicated. I mentally apologized over and over and over to my heavenly Father for succumbing to the temptations I excitedly and willingly partook in.

My whole life, I had been avoiding drinking and sexual sin. I was not going to turn out like my parents. I swore in my life I would not make the same choices.

Those months I felt like I was making up for lost time. My standard of truth became a "screw it" attitude. But even in those moments of covenant violations, I never felt whole. I never felt right. I never felt like what I had been missing was really being found. Maybe that is why this particular confession felt so important to me. My existence was not found in trying to end the past I could not get rid of, but the future I needed to keep fighting for.

Why don't we talk about this more as women? Why is this an unspoken conversation of excommunicated women from the Church of Jesus Christ of Latter-Day Saints? Well, I am talking about it now. I am talking about women that, like me, made mindful choices and lost our memberships.

I did not want this. I wanted and, still to this day, desire to be a member of the church. I recognized the good the church was and still is. I recognized that for me, the legacy I had been given from those that came before me was real and kept me from harm's way for most of my childhood. I was ashamed I had thrown it all away. And for what? Trying to figure out what I already knew? That marrying the first guy that paid any attention to me and gave me false value was really going to work? Come on, Elizabeth. You are smarter than that!

There was no one to blame for this but me. I had to face that fact. No one was going to save me. I had known that for a long time. As my eyes peeled back to the carpeted wall, I knew now was the moment I had to face reality that the only one I have ever been able to rely on was staring me back in the face. Why did Jesus look like He was smiling?

For the first time in a long time, I was without words. Nothing would come out of my mouth. I continued to look straight through the bishop at that picture of Jesus as he tried to express the Savior's concern for me. He began to list the things I was no longer allowed to do: some of them obvious, and some not so much. But I didn't care. I wasn't listening. I was no longer a member of the Church of Jesus Christ of Latter-Day Saints.

I could not explain it then as I look back, and I can hardly explain it now. As though I had just been reciting the tale of someone else's tragedy, I sat straight up, squared my shoulders, sniffed one last time, stopped crying, stopped feeling sorry for myself, and quietly threw away my used and disgusting tissues in the small beige trash can next to me.

Electricity could not have reached me faster. No matter what the bishop kept saying about the rules of being excommunicated, this strange surge of hope and love continued to penetrate my existence. I did not allow the feeling to leave. I hugged the emotion of sorrow and hope together and merged their existence into one. I felt conflicted with the optimistic second chance just handed me and the inappropriate behavior I spent the better part of the evening verbally throwing up.

In a situation where there was an excommunication, I imagined a typical response might be falling into the fetal position and wailing uncontrollably. I figured the body would convulsively fall to the floor, and the person would have to be helped up and escorted out of the building, flailing in a paralysis state. Or I imagined a person so angry and full of hate that there would be swearing and name-calling projected loudly and obnoxiously in the direction of the bishopric as though it was their personal fault.

I imagined that after the disciplinary counsel, a person would most likely cry for days upon end, like I witnessed my mom do on the floor of our filthy house in her hoarder-style bedroom, surrounded by eight small helpless children. She was at the pinnacle of her manic-depressive state after my dad had left her. We learned quickly how to survive and fend for ourselves. My mom did not shower, eat, cook a meal, or leave her room to do more than use the bathroom.

Even to this day, I struggle with other women, especially mother-like figures. At the age of fourteen, I was raising seven siblings, aged one to twelve. Both of my parents had mentally checked out of their parental responsibilities so naturally, the role of caregiver fell on me. I hated it. I hated my mom. I hated my dad. I continued to hold on to resentment for years and used my rough childhood experiences as blame for some of the choices I recently made. I blamed my dad for not teaching me how to find a "good guy" to make a home with. I blamed my mom for neglecting me so much I didn't know the very basics of housework, hard work, and not creating or feeding into drama.

I mothered my siblings while my mom sat in a mental health hospital for attempting suicide. This "mothering" continued for several years until I realized nothing was going to change. I moved out on my own and bounced from friend's house to friend's house. I slept on couches, floors, and the back seat of a car.

I found a way to high school every day. I was determined to graduate. I decided I would have steady attendance at a new ward away from my mom and found that connection with the members is what kept my faith growing. I was not going to be helpless like my mom. I was not going to be untouchable like my dad. I was going to learn how to take care of myself, spiritually and physically. I told myself that no matter what or how hard it might get, I would do everything opposite of how I was raised. I wanted to be something in life.

I had battled feelings of worthlessness and self-pity on a daily basis but successfully hid it away from the people closest to me in hopes that they would assume that the "nothing" I felt I was, was actually "something."

However, as I sat in the bishop's office on that most catastrophic night, I realized I had become just like the woman I hated the most, my mom. I sat in that chair with reality slapping me square in the face and the inability to stop the "nothingness" from filling my very soul. I was finally nothing, like I had been told by my mom, my dad, my abusers, my ex, and now my bishop.

Yet a contradictory thought crept passionately and stealthily into my core. I was not "nothing." What was happening? What is this feeling? It felt...good? Is this right? Am I supposed to feel "something." Am I actually feeling like I am "something"? How is this possible?

I felt strong. I felt confident. I felt as though I had finally received the antibiotics for the infection I could not cure by myself. It was instantaneous! And even though I could not explain it, I knew I was going to be okay. Being excommunicated was just the gift I needed.

While the tears continued to fall from all three men, the bishop stopped talking and looked at me with a father-like compassion. He asked me if I had any questions. "No," I said as I looked up with a confident side grin. For the first time in hours, all three men looked up at me with direct eye contact.

I had their attention. I had the floor.

They appeared as though they were scared I was going to burst into words of anger and emotionally abuse them. Then, with all the love and confidence I could muster, the scared looks subsided as I began my final words of the evening meeting.

"I will be back. I will not be excommunicated long. I have a testimony of my Savior, and I know that the actions I have done were mine, by my own choices, and that they were wrong. I also know that I am not excommunicated because God is mad at me or wants to get back at me. I know it is because He loves me, and this was my wake-up call. While this is not the news I wanted to hear, I knew it was the decision that was going to be made. I also know that this was not easy for any of you, and I took you away from your families tonight to be here with me. That means a lot to me. I know you did not ask for this calling, yet here you are. Brethren, if we have nothing else to discuss, I would like to excuse myself. I have a lot of repenting to do."

They did not say a word. The room was completely quiet as I stood up to leave. The men were obviously awestruck at my response to the impending crisis. Then, with confusion in the air, the bishop spoke. "Elizabeth," he paused. I continued to stand.

"You are not 'nothing.' You are everything to your heavenly Father." He paused again as I stood there and allowed the words to sink in.

I couldn't believe that of all the words and emotions I expressed in that very long encounter that he remembered the first comment I had made. I told all three of them that I was tired of feeling like I was "nothing" to anyone. I told them I wanted to feel something again, and all the fighting, neglect, and abuse had left me with the only conclusion my mind could muster. I had to be "nothing" because if I was really anything of consequence, I would have had a better childhood, the knowledge of how to pick a better husband, and the strength to leave situations before they got bad. I was now being told, as a final statement of parting, that I was wrong again. I was not "nothing." Those were not the bishop's words. I knew they came from a higher place. I knew it the minute they left his shaking lips.

I nodded in respect to the sentiment and thoughtful closure and opened the office door, determined never to return in these circumstances again. I don't know where all that confidence came from. I was more embarrassed than I had ever been in my life and was trying to not let the anger of embarrassment I felt overshadow this moment.

Who had I just become? I was no longer the Elizabeth from three hours ago. For the first time in my life, I felt the surge of feeling like I was something to someone. I liked this new girl. I knew from this moment on, if I could just hold onto the shirt tails of this new "Elizabeth," I might make it. I just might be okay after all.

I went home that night with a very cloudy brain. My thoughts would not stay still. I was processing the entirety of the evening's events in broken slideshow moments. I figured out I had an unrealistic time frame I could live by and find myself back in full membership.

I found myself in quick moments with powerful surges of hope and dedication to recovery of my soul and then longer moments of despair and grief.

I remembered a comment I learned in a Sunday school class years ago about repenting and being truly sincere. "Are you sorry because you got caught and are really being cornered into repenting, or are you sorry because you humbled yourself before the Lord and allowed Him to help you catch yourself?"

The fact that I was the one that approached my ecclesiastical leaders and told my story with complete understanding and willingness to accept my fate kept bringing me back to the surge of hope I so desperately needed. It was like I was drowning in my thoughts, unable to breathe, being sent rescue breaths through some sort of spiritual CPR. I was dying, and I knew it. I wasn't willing to just lay there and take it. My physical body succumbed to the spiritual pain I felt. I could not stop crying with my mind having memory seizures of my moral crime, then more crying and more mind racing.

I just sat on my couch in my living room. I didn't even shut my front door. It was late, no lights were turned on. It was cold. I was exhausted both mentally and physically. I stared at my pink flip phone. I knew I had to call my ex. We were still married on paper, even though the marriage was no more.

My ex had his mom dropped the kids off a few moments after I returned home. I had left the door open behind her. My two beautiful babies were tucked safely into their temporary beds, sleeping to the terrible sounds of my sobbing. I wanted so much more for them than a mother full of sin and sorrow. I wanted to be the mother I never had, and yet, here I was, performing the role of inadequacy at Oscar status.

I had no self-esteem. I knew I could get through this. I just didn't know how. I bounced back and forth between glimmers of courage and moments of utter despair. I had allowed men to come into my life as a way to feel valued. There was no value to be found in what their pretenses were. I quickly plummeted into depression.

Most of that night was spent reviewing the last two-and-a-half years. I married the guy that got me pregnant because of advice I received from an ecclesiastical leader stating I would never be forgiven unless I made the situation "right." I tried to make the situation acceptable to myself and God, but I could not prevail, for either myself or God. I had been trying to get the acceptance of men my whole life.

Again, to no prevail. I finally understood the phrase "daddy issues" as I was witnessing what unresolved distortions of self can and, in fact, lead to. I felt my only hope for continuing this nightmare was to just get through it. I could not get through this without taking actual action and facing the demons. Hell would have been more welcoming.

My ex was physically and verbally abusive, a narcissist, and a terrible liar (all toxic behavioral traits). He had had an affair while we were married and got the other woman pregnant. We had an all-out custody battle with evaluators, expert witnesses, and such large legal fees I still, to this day, doubt I will ever recover financially.

At the end of it all, after years and years of court, the judge found the father of my two older children to be "more religiously compatible" than I was. How? I don't know. But I knew that if Christ could not have a fair trial, why should I expect one? My ex would end up with full custody for the next ten years.

I thought my life was hard up until that point. But losing my kids and not understanding why was a hit no mother could come back from. As I was working for DCFS at the time, I was going into homes and removing children for abuse and neglect. This was second nature to me, considering my own upbringing. What I could not understand is how I could have lost custody of my own children? I had done nothing illegal that could justify their new placement, not like the mothers I was taking kids away from for a living. It was a painful reminder of the legal injustice in the world today, and that unless you had money to burn, you would never get a fair shake in the legal system.

I went to work every day only to return to an empty house. I had to force myself physically out of bed and shower every day. A coworker I confided in was so patient with me and my self-pity. I imagine I must have been emotionally draining on everyone that would listen to my story.

One day in the midst of my complaining about my life story, starting with the blame and finger pointing to my mother, she quietly glanced at me with compassion and said, "You should be thanking your mom because you would not be who you are today without the trials she created for you." She then continued with pure doctrine validating her statement, "2 Nephi 2:2, 'And he shall consecrate thine afflictions for thy gain.'" Like President Eyring cautioned, I was worried about the wrong problem.

I was publicly embarrassed in my small community by my situation. But it was not the public that embarrassed me. It was my own assault on my soul for which I stood ashamed. I had few friends and no extended family here. I was utterly and desperately alone. I thoroughly understood the small-town dynamic and cultural references to religion.

The clarity of concise understanding that, once again, men had acted in the name of God without consideration of God's intentions helped me separate what I knew to be true about my faith from how others behaved in the name of faith. This important distinction kept me going to church, renewing my commitment to God, and changing my lifestyle choices.

Going to church was embarrassing, but I kept going. I had to decline any request to pray or comment. I could not take the sacrament or bear my testimony. I concluded that part of being embarrassed was part of the repentance process.

Repentance is a commandment, not a request. "How hard to bear you know not" (D&C 19:15). There is nothing wrong with feeling uncomfortable as that is where change takes place. If I did not feel uncomfortable about my situation, how would I ever be able to sincerely change?

And how I wanted change. Before my eyes, I started to see myself changing for the better. The purge of my excuses was a start. My willingness to take on the personal embarrassment and buckle down was the next move.

I found this feeling comparable to a referee at a basketball game being yelled at by fans. Most referees just ignore the insults and push forward in the moment of trying to make the best calls they have been trained to do. Most referees remain unbiased in their calls despite the ignorant comments slung their way. And despite all the hurtful and meaningless words being yelled when the ref makes a call hurtful to the team being called on, they keep going. They keep calling, and they keep trying to be unbiased.

I became the referee of my own actions and had to learn to ignore the criticism of ignorant bystanders. I had to keep going. I had to keep a straight face.

I had to learn to embrace the "first things first" principle: "Seek ye first the kingdom of God." An important characteristic of our loving Father in heaven is the calm nature in which He imputes His cleansing fire. I felt guilt as I appropriately should have. Guilt became a trigger warning for me to know that I was walking too close to the edge of sin again. I embarrassed guilt as a direct call to repentance and ownership of my behavior. I was owning my impact.

It would have been way too easy to have just walked away from everything. I had seen what taking the easy route did to my loved ones. I was not going to throw my hands up in the air and say I was giving up. I was going to run to repentance.

I did not want to train my emotions to give up. I had devoted all my existence to being a better person than what was taught to me. My marriage had ended, but it never should have begun. That choice was on me. I had to take ownership of how I got to this place to begin with. That meant reaching into my painful back story and remembering why I started my journey to be better. I revisit those memories often as a way to help push me through my tough times.

The night I was excommunicated, I eventually made it to my bedroom floor. I fell to my knees in prayer. My mind was so loud with thoughts of how I was going to recover emotionally, financially, physically, and spiritually from all this. All I wanted was a friend, someone who could see my worth, someone who didn't want anything from me as I had nothing to give. I just wanted a friend.

Within twenty-four hours, my prayer was answered.

Deputy Pete Allred had learned that I was not doing well emotionally and called to check on me. He worked as a deputy police officer with the county, and we had worked on a few cases together. He had heard I was going through "some stuff" and just wanted to check on me. I cannot begin to tell how that one bit of concern he shared with me saved my life.

At first, I was mortified by the thought that the rumors of my behavior had already made the front-page gossip news. Then I mentally questioned his intentions. I didn't want to get into another relationship with someone who threw puppy dog eyes at me and told me everything I wanted and, frankly, needed to hear. I had to get healthy, strong, emotionally comfortable with myself before allowing myself into another relationship.

Pete's willingness to allow me to heal and accept me for what I was going through proved to be an unexpected challenge for the both of us. He was a handsome, single guy, never married, no kids, and a good standing member of the church. What did he want with me? I never felt pretty, I had a failed first marriage with two little kids I did not have custody of, and was just excommunicated. There had to be something wrong with him that he even thought I was worth the time to call and check on me.

We had never had a conversation prior to that first call that was not about a child abuse case. He had a good reputation, and I did not. He was born and raised in this county and had family all over. He was related to what seemed like everyone. Surely, someone would have told him of my local mishaps.

We started talking about life and family, what our life goals were, and what we expected out of humanity. One weekend, we decided we were both hungry and decided food would be a good option to indulge in. We were not dating, just "hanging out" as friends. I had been extra cautious of my interactions with others. I did not really understand myself, nor did I trust myself to be able to interact appropriately with the opposite sex. I knew I needed time to understand personal boundaries and enforce standards I had grown up learning about but never really implemented. Pete gave me that space and time to develop an adult understanding of what chastity really meant.

While driving the hour and a half to the lunch spot we had agreed on, the shallow surface level conversations we had been used to developed into an in-depth conversation of where the other one was at spiritually.

This had been a conversation I had been dreading. Pete did not know I had been excommunicated yet, and I was scared to tell him for fear he would no longer want to be my friend, a confidant, or a "hang out buddy."

It started out with a question about going to church with him. My soul sank as I knew the minute the sacrament was passed, I would have to refuse, and my sins exposed. The insecurities of my past life slowly crept into my mind. Here was the lifelong battle of worthiness laughing in my ear as I sat in this car with no escape at seventy miles an hour, reiterating that I would never be good enough for anyone. The battle for the affection of the male gender had been put on hold, but I did not want to lose the one friend I had. Being honest was risky. Lying was risky. I had not been one to mince words in the past, but exposing Pete to the personal radiation I had been consumed by meant he had a choice to stay or leave. I did not want him to find my soul repulsive. I wanted him to see my broken and healing heart.

I went back and forth in my mind questioning what to say. I no longer had the gift of the Holy Ghost to guide me but knew and believed the Spirit was present to lead. What should I say? The awkward silence had become exhausting. The thought finally came to me that if I could not own up to my current situation now, when would I? If I was going to be given the gift of a friend (and I felt Pete was a gift of friendship I had asked for and been given), then what would I need to do?

Part of the repentant process for an individual is letting go of what you cannot control. I knew I could not control the disappointment Pete would feel when I would eventually cut the artery of truth and bleed my honesty on him. I wanted to soften the blow, but how do you stop the fast pitch of "I have been excommunicated." What baseball mitt can stop the strike without the sound of the hit?

I desperately wanted to keep my friend. I wanted to protect him from my ugly, broken reality of what I had become. But I knew that in the long run, a friendship was based on truth. A love was based on honesty. If Jesus Christ was going to accept me back in His loving grasp, I had to let go of the fear Satan had imitated as confidence for years.

Pete had to know the truth of who I was, what I was going through, and be allowed to choose for himself who he wanted to be associated with in his own life's journey. I could not, and would not, be allowed to falsify my intentions to lead him to believe I was something other than what I really was. And what I was, was a broken, repentant, daughter of God that had made a serious decision to work on my relationship with Christ first. I had to put Him first. I had to allow Him to guide me to where I needed to be and not force the path of repentance to form the way I wanted, but what He wanted.

I had to be willing to accept whatever Pete decided after letting him hear my truth. It was so painful. I had grown to love our time together and our free honesty. I had to live up to what I had proclaimed to be, sorry for what I had done.

As the focus word of the sentence, "excommunicated," left my mouth half an hour into the hour and a half ride home, his gaze went from the side of me to the front window. He looked forward in the passenger seat in silence, not making a sound, a stir, or a sigh. His silence was hurtful, but unintentional. What did I expect? A pat on the back? Condolences? A hug? I had just told him I had taken everything he held sacred and true and threw it in the garbage. Excommunicated was one thing, but a *woman* excommunicated was a completely different conversation.

His face was motionless. I kept looking for signs of acceptance to what I had just said, but he sat stone still for an hour. I did not say anything else past the sentence of being excommunicated as I felt I had already said too much, yet not enough.

Fifteen miles before we reached his house, I felt the strong impression, not necessarily to offer an explanation, but tell him how I was currently feeling. I started out by telling Pete I had a love for my Savior that could not be shaken. I told him I still loved the gospel and was working through the repentance process with my bishop who I admired and respected fully. I reiterated that while he might feel I had let him down, I had not sinned against him. I had not violated a convent with him, and I had no intention of hiding my truth from him. I ended with letting him know I enjoyed the last month we had spent together and respected his decision if he did not want to spend time with me anymore. He offered no statement in return, just continued the awkward silence of contemplation.

By the time I had pulled my car into his driveway, I had no hope he would want to continue our friendship. As the car went into park, he opened the door, said bye, and walked to his front door, not looking back. I sat silently still in the car for a few seconds as I watched him walk in his front door and not look back. The stillness of the inside of the car forced me to put the car into reverse and drive back to my lonely apartment.

That night, Satan found my thoughts and used them like play-dough to control my sense of worthiness. I could not put myself together emotionally and understood his laughing I had been hearing in my head was going to continue throughout the rest of my existence. Satan was such a bully to my self-esteem. He continued to mock the idea that I would never know what true love or friendship could be, and that I needed to just accept my fate of failure in this life. The struggle of thinking that if I ever got close to anyone, I would have to continue to go through that humiliation over and over became so powerful and overwhelming.

No longer having the gift of the Holy Ghost was like losing a limb and experiencing phantom pains. I knew he used to be there, but I could no longer feel him like I had taken for granted my entire life. The absence of the constant companionship was manifested in full force. I had once had a friend that I enjoyed the comfort of, but by choosing to ignore his promptings, I had subjected my soul to the thorns of a rose bush. The scraping of pain had overtaken the softness of the voice of guidance.

Asking for comfort became a moment-to-moment encounter. Forcing my mind to allow peace became an exhausting workout. Forcing the expulsion of negative thinking had now become the reality of what I would now be faced with until I proved to the Lord I had truly repented and wanted the blessings back I had previously deemed as worthless.

I went to bed that evening with newly filled bags under my eyes, tear-soaked tissues, and exhausted by the debates I had been having with myself.

Morning could not have come soon enough.

My little pink cell phone startled me awake as it rang over and over to the tune of some hip-hop rapper. I let it go to voicemail, assuming it was my ex asking for a fight I had no strength to encounter.

A few minutes later, it rang again. Again, I let it go to voicemail.

This time, without a pause, the text alert notified me that someone wanted my attention despite wanting to be left alone to my self-pity. I crawled out of bed to the wall my phone was plugged into and peeled it open.

My eyes could not have been seeing straight as two missed calls from Pete lit up. Then the text: "What ya doing? You awake?"

Pause…

Pause again…

What?

What was this?

What was going to be my response? Do I call him back? Do I text him back?

What would I even say? Was there an answer or explanation I needed to offer to a question I left on his doorstep yesterday?

Not knowing what I should say or do, I left the phone on the floor and ran to my bathroom sink to splash cold water on my sorrow-filled face. I put myself together as much as I could muster without trying to look or sound desperate and ran back to my phone. I unplugged it from the wall and skipped (emotionally, not physically) into my living room.

"What's up?" I texted back.

Not knowing how long he would take to respond, I threw a Pop-Tart into the toaster. But before I could even press the button down, he responded, "Wanna come over?"

I checked myself for excitement for fear I would blow this encounter with desperation in my response. I counted to 100. "Sure, what are you doing?" I asked. I pulled my Pop-Tart out of the toaster oven and set it on my paper towel.

"Nothing, just want to hang out before I have to go to work tonight."

I left the hot Pop-Tart on the counter, grabbed my purse and keys, and left the apartment with the same mental skipping I had just given to my living room.

I arrived at Pete's house twenty minutes later. As I pulled into the driveway, I saw him standing in his opened front door with a look of content and calmness. I felt so confused and excited that my friend had not left me, nor given up on me. Pete left the door open for me as he walked into the front room of his house, allowing me to shut the door behind myself.

Pete saw me for what I was trying so hard to become. He saw the new "Elizabeth" that was trying her best to change. It had not been a quiet night for him, he later told me, as he thought about what the scary and unknown adventure I had set myself on. He challenged his own knowledge of what it meant for someone to be excommunicated and whether or not he wanted to embark on that journey as a person of support and reassurance.

Pete knew he had several other options available to him in terms of dating and friendships but told me he wanted to see me through this and felt I could. He explained that my words of love for my Savior rang true to his heart as we drove uncomfortably home the day before. If the atonement could be true for one, it had to be true for all. After all, he explained, God was not a respecter of persons, and the whole point of this life is to abandon all our worldly sins, repent, and come follow Him. Pete shared that he had never met anyone before that had gone through the excommunication process and wanted to help any way he could.

I knew in an instant I had met my champion. Pete would soon prove to be my biggest cheerleader and defender. He chose to stay.

As our friendship grew, our love blossomed. He was so patient with my flaws. I had to relearn how to be in a relationship with any-one, and he stayed with me the whole time.

I remember the first time he told me he loved me. I remember our first kiss. I knew he was to be trusted. He was the first man to ever show me the respect I knew I deserved.

He asked me to marry him shortly after nine months of dating. We had a small family-only ceremony in the backyard of his sister's house. My two small children were there and saw the beginning of our new forever.

To this day, I don't know why he stuck around. I was brutally honest with him about what I was going through. He didn't have to stay. If he wanted someone to spend the rest of his life with, baggage free, I was not his flight. But he paid the price with me, and I still get those sweet and tender butterflies when I see him.

He taught me so much about who I really was and not to believe what I thought I had to be based on what my past told me I had no choice in becoming. I learned that I raised my hand in the preexistence and said, "Yes! I agree to come to this life and fail miserably! Sign me up! It doesn't matter the cost. I want in!"

I still get butterflies when I think of Pete because of the love and selflessness he has for me. I felt like Joseph Smith when he saw his friends and embraced them. "These are my boys!"

I learned I needed to stop expecting others to provide for me emotionally. I had to take care of myself first.

I learned I was a spiritual bulimic. I ate it all up on Sunday and threw it up on Monday.

I learned that even though I know I'm not perfect, I was enough for Pete and my children.

I learned I was holding onto the trauma of my childhood and letting it make all my unhealthy life choices.

I learned that fairness does not mean equal. But most importantly, I learned it was time for me to grow up.

So I let the little hurt Elizabeth go. She couldn't stay. The evil things that had happened to her could no longer be in charge of making life decisions.

It was not easy, and anyone who has ever been here knows. It was a process and progress still in the making. I could not, and would not, move forward and find happiness until I started saying what I wasn't saying. I had to shut up about stuff that did not matter anymore. A lot of people have painful pasts. Some worse than mine, and while everyone is different, I had to stop comparing my worst self to someone else's best self.

Pete was my beginning to the end I so desperately needed. I was being given freedom, and I needed to learn to be comfortable with being uncomfortable, the only place change can happen.

After three years of being without church membership and the painful loss of the Holy Ghost to comfort my lost soul, I entered the waters of baptism and met Pete in the half-filled, cold-water font. I held his arm and my nose as I reentered those sacred waters a second time with a new passion for repentance. As much as I loved having a second baptism, I also hated the fact that I had put myself in the position to be rebaptized. I was out of "time-out!" But it came at the cost of self-inflicted indignation. It did not have to be this way. I should have just listened to what I always knew to be true.

Yet, wishing to go back in time and change the choices that cannot be changed is fruitless for anyone. Scene one: I failed. Fade to black. Scene two: the atonement of Jesus Christ. Fade to credits!

After Moses learned his true identity as the son of God, he felt transformed and spiritually powerful, yet physically weak. Pouncing on the opportunity to take advantage of Moses's weakness, Satan appeared and offered Moses the chance to be rich with the things of the world by simple worship. Moses now knew *who* he was. Satan offered a faux and cheap imitation to the power of God. Moses did not fail. He held on to the knowledge of who he really was and what his worth really meant. The imitation could not compare.

I had learned the stupid and hard way that the imitation does not compare to the real deal! The spirit of God cannot be replaced by what the world says is happiness. I now know firsthand that wickedness never was happiness. I know this because I have felt the real love of God and the fake acceptance of Satan and the two never shall meet. They can't. There is only one or the other: real love or fake acceptance. We cannot serve two masters. Moses had it figured out. Wishing I would have figured it out before learning the lesson does me no good. I have come to accept what was and let it go. That choice was hard, but it has allowed me many more victories in my life than failures.

CHAPTER 4

AFTER YEARS OF LISTENING TO hundreds of disclosures of abuse, I have become even more firm in my belief that every little girl deserves the safe space of her father's arms. Every little girl should be allowed to lay down next to her father and cuddle in the safest and unsexualized way possible. Girls need dads. Girls need *safe* dads. This world needs more men to step up and be that safe place for their daughters.

If there is one great thing I remember about my own father, despite his flaws, I knew I was always safe in his arms. I have a picture of every one of my siblings cuddling safely in the arms of my father as they napped together in peace. I cherish those moments with my dad and feel blessed every day that the world could stop and peace could be found in the arms of my father. I was blessed to have those moments. But too many of the children I interview will never know what it's like to fall asleep in the arms of their father and not be woken up by fear or pain.

In one memorable interview that made me lose sleep for weeks, RB disclosed that every man in her life had sexually abused her in the most loving way possible. It was the physical abuse that bothered her. And when asked the details of the sexual abuse, her response struck a nerve in my brain, refusing to let me feel any compassion for the pedophiles in her life. RB led into her disclosure with the disturbing sentiment that she was touched by all these men "the only way a guy can touch a girl."

In RB's young mind, men only touch little girls in one way. And it's not the gentle cuddles every child deserves from every trusted father figure in their lives.

If men don't step up and realize their significant role in the development and growth of children in this world, I'm going to lose my mind and start something on fire or throw a brick at someone's face. Actually, I can't do that. My supervisor told me that was not acceptable behavior, so I have to act professional. So I guess in that case, I will just write a book and demand fathers start showing up for their daughters.

One of the greatest examples I have seen of how this can be done (so I know it is possible) was not only my own father, but also from what I have seen my husband Pete do with our own children. I have relished witnessing Pete fall asleep with our babies in his arms. My daughters are constantly finding solace under the arm of their father wrapped gently over their shoulders while he wiped their tears. Their experiences of sitting on Pete's lap while he sings along with a Disney princess or reading for the fifth time "No, David!" will be ingrained in their minds as it has mine forever.

Pete learned this from his own father, John. My first experience in meeting John was quite comical. I was invited to finally be introduced to his parents as the reason Pete was finally smiling, laughing, and happy again. The pressure was huge for me.

Pete was a single, never married, no kid thirty-two-year-old Mormon guy in small-town Utah. The pressure he had been receiving for years to get married and settle down had become so astronomical it had become unbearable for him. He was the oldest of four children. All his siblings had been married years ago with children of their own. Pete was the fun uncle that could come and go as he pleased but had to endure the countless blind dates and conversations of which girl his siblings thought he should try to connect with. Dating was becoming a burden for him, the older he got. The women he was being set up with started to come with more and more baggage.

His sister told me a few years after Pete and I were married how much he would proclaim at family functions when cornered by all the married couples trying to set him up with someone that he would never date, let alone marry someone that already had kids. She stated she loved seeing us together because Pete was able to see the good in a person despite their flaws. She welcomed me into her family with opened arms and no judgements. So when he announced to his family that we were dating, I became the "dropped jaw," "no words," "pause in disbelief" to everything they ever thought they knew.

It wasn't until Pete met the queen of baggage (that's me) that his mindset changed on what he really wanted in a wife. I was introduced to his family as his dream girl, the woman he always envisioned to be the wife he always wanted, and the mother of his children. No pressure, right?

In my mind, I was never going to measure up to the person he was describing to his family. I was every disappointment, failure, and dysfunctional adult I had been painted to be by my childhood experiences and previous marriage. I had become the product of my raising and would never be deserving of the future Pete was offering me. I would never experience what a solid, healthy family felt like and was destined for depression knocking on my door.

But Pete made me look in the mirror of my reality to see my worth and soul as he saw me. He picked up my scattered puzzle pieces, glued me back together, and presented me as the kintsugi I was.

So here I stood. Insecurities and all, being presented as the love of his life to a family that had no idea what emotional tornado I was about to blow into their lives.

John was laying on the floor of his living room with several little boys no more than three years old, trying to wrestle him to the ground. The boys were covered in smiles as their sweaty red bodies jumped, wrangled, and twisted to hold down one of John's arms as he held his position to the wool rug positioned perfectly in front of the homemade fireplace mantel built by Pete's grandfather. The giggles continued as Pete's mother, Dianne, scolded John for being too rough with the boys. The granddaughters were in the open concept kitchen with Dianne baking the world's best desserts to be presented before, during, and after dinner. I learned quickly there was no rule in Dianne's house that you had to eat your dinner first before you could have dessert. In the home of the world's best grandma, dessert was always available.

Had I died? Was this the la-la land everyone talked about? Where was I?

No one was fighting or hateful. No one was rude or drunk. People were kind, and kids were being allowed to be kids.

Did this world really exist, and if so, how did I get here? Did I deserve to be here? Would this moment last?

Thank the good Lord it did! This world does exist and is available for everyone! I'm serious. After all these years, I can attest that there is still good in the world, and good people and families are thriving.

Several years after Pete and I were married, my custody battle with my ex came to an end. When my daughter decided she had had enough of her dad's lies and manipulation, she made the choice to live with Pete and me.

This devastating hit to my ex's ego caused him to lash out at my oldest son. He threatened to kill himself if my son left to live with me too.

On a weekend visit, my son and I had an insightful talk about choices. I explained to my son that his dad's choices belonged to just that his dad. My son would never be responsible if his dad chose to take his own life.

My son was a freshman in high school at the time and knew that if he was going to ever have a chance to live with Pete and I, the door was wide open, and he would have to step through. The ability for my son, as young as he was, to have to make such a life-changing decision helped me to see him in a light of maturity. He took on challenges with determination. He made better life choices than his dad, or I had previously shown him. His soft and tender heart helped him be a leader in school and look after those that were teased, bullied, or less fortunate.

My son made several comments over phone calls to his dad that showed intentions of righteousness. When his dad would cry, plead, beg, yell at, or try to humiliate him into returning back to his care, my son would quickly respond with founded rhetoric of fact.

My older children's strength became an example to me. Pete and I grew our family through the ongoing challenges of blending a family. We had three children together. These adorable little half siblings to my older kids created a sense of family togetherness for all of us. My two older kids wanted a two-parent home. At this point, only Pete and I could offer this.

I was beginning to get burned out at DCFS. I knew it was time to take a pause when the administrative side of my work started to interfere with the safety of the children I was trying to save.

The moment I knew I needed a break came when one of my clients died. I had been working the case for months, and the cute little eight-year-old boy was the only child to two drug-addicted parents. The parents were receiving their drugs in the legal way, medical doctors, but were being overprescribed. The little boy's basic needs were being met, but my concern that the parents were too strung out to really nurture and care for him fell on deaf ears. I pleaded with my supervisor to let me petition for a removal. The little boy had been seen playing in the apartment complex parking lot until 10:30 p.m. on a school night. He went to school in filthy clothes and smelled of not bathing in months. My request was met with a denial explaining that "at least he is going to school" and "at least he has clothes to wear and a place to sleep."

As I was driving to work one day, I was met with an unusual traffic stop right before a turn into town. I noticed several police vehicles and ambulances. This early in the morning to have this extreme response to what I thought was just a fender bender spiked my curiosity. I called my police associates to ask what was all the commotion, and no one answered. After waiting twenty minutes for the traffic to dissipate, I was able to move my vehicle and proceed into work. Off to my left, as I passed what I minimized as a fender bender and saw the complete accident, there laying off the side of the road was a tiny body covered in a white sheet. The car was unrecognizable, but the woman I saw sitting in the back of the patrol car was none other than the mother of my client.

Her face was pressed into the inside of the car window, scream-ing and crying. Her son, my eight-year-old client, was dead.

The mother had followed her pain meds with half a bottle of Vodka, managed to wake up her son, stumble to the car, and attempt to drive him to school. As she was driving around the bend out of town at ridiculous speeds, her red 1985 Buick Riviera rolled four times before coming to a stop. My little eight-year-old client had been thrown from the vehicle and, in its roll, landed upside down on his little frame, killing him instantly. Mom lived with no scratches.

I quit the next week.

I knew I would be back, just…I needed a break.

While I was five months pregnant with my second daughter, Pete and I were sealed in the temple for time and all eternity with my two-year-old son sitting at the altar with us. We were sealed forever. The interesting memory of emotion regarding that event was the differing feelings I had between the three times I have been sealed to someone in the temple.

First, my parents. I had no idea what was going on and felt indifferent about the events inside the temple. I just wanted my fam-ily to be nice to each other and hoped for a new outcome to the already ensuing chaos.

Second, my ex. I had anticipated that a marriage in the temple would yield positive results. The feeling I had of confusion and hes-itation had more insight than impact in retrospect. I could not, for the life of me, figure out why I would have the feelings of "pause" when I was driving to the temple to be sealed to my ex. I was doing the "right" thing. I was going to the temple to be sealed to a worthy priesthood holder, so the feelings of "wrong" made no sense to me. I brushed them off as nerves and ignored what I now know were clearly promptings.

Third, Pete. The obvious difference to me was that I could not get to the temple fast enough to be sealed to Pete. It was so night and day different from the feelings I had when being sealed to my ex and the indifference I felt when being sealed to my parents. With Pete, I would have run to the temple if I did not have a car to drive me there. There was no pause. There was no hesitation. There was no questioning or doubt! There was only urgency in love. I finally understood what true love was, and I wanted it forever. I knew the only place to ensure I would have eternity with Pete and all my children was in the temple. Heaven help the person, place, or thing that tried to stop me from getting there!

As our marriage progressed through the years, it did not come without challenges. My older kids and I picked up our broken pieces and tried to glue ourselves back together in our new life. Like Pete and I had to learn how to be healthy in a relationship, my older kids also had to learn how to be parented by a mentally healthy father figure. My son embraced the change with minor occurrences. My daughter, not so much. It was more difficult for her to trust Pete based solely of how she had been treated by her father. My inability to protect her still wears on me. With my hands tied by the legal system, there was only so much a mother could do other than offer love and support in any way allowable.

My oldest daughter quickly became my sidekick and helped me with the younger kids. She was a natural at caring for others. She showed compassion and humor, which helped her build a relationship of trust with them. They loved her so much. They looked up to her and still do. I relied on her a lot while I tried to balance the working life with the mothering life. Pete and I had little to no chance of financially recovering from the debt the last ten years of legal battles presented to us. I worked as much as I could to just make ends meet.

I knew I had to get a better-paying job and decided to try my skills at a master's degree. I worked on every assignment with integrity and passion. There were many sleepless nights as I worked full time during the day and wrote my assignments into the night. Four o'clock in the morning found me writing with one hand as I held my newborn baby in my left arm. I enjoyed my addiction to crystal-light-energy packets just to get through a few more hours of parenting and paper writing.

After two years of dedicated working, schooling, and mothering, my diploma arrived in the mail. I did not want to walk or attend the graduation ceremony. I didn't need the accolades. I just needed to know that I could do it.

I put that degree in the nicest frame I could afford and hung it above the fireplace mantel. I was so proud of my accomplishment. I wanted my kids to see the dedication and know they too could someday do hard things.

But doing one hard thing does not mean we are except for further sorrow. My degree would not make me immune to life's challenges. If anything, my challenges got harder.

CHAPTER 5

WHAT DOES A BROKEN WOMAN need? Are we ever really fixed?

The Japanese have a beautiful ideology called kintsugi or golden joinery. When something breaks, it is joined back together with gold, and the value actually increases. But what if you have no gold, or you feel you have no worth?

In 2012, I got a call from my mom a little before midnight. I let it go to voicemail. That was the worst voicemail I ever received.

My mom, very frankly, said my brother Mike shot himself in the head.

I flew out to Georgia from Utah at 3:00 a.m. and sat by his hospital bedside for three days while the nurses continued to stabilize his bodily organs to retrieve them for donations to eight recipients.

This was the kid I raised. This was the kid I loved, my brother who loved everyone more than himself. But the perfect storm of drugs, alcohol, a fight with his girlfriend, and chronic depression finally found its way into the black powder of a bullet pulled by the trigger of aloneness and a sense of never being good enough.

When I arrived in Georgia, I was greeted by grief and overwhelmed by the reality of my situation. My mom tried and tried to apologize to me as though she was the one that held the gun to his head and pulled the trigger. She was accepting her poor attempts at motherhood in an effort to thwart any possible blame thrown in her direction. But she never could stop a bullet. Sometimes, she was the one that shot the bullet. But not this time. This time, it was Mike.

And it was his way of saying he felt so alone and unloved by anyone. For Mike, it was the first time he finished something he started. And yet, he left everything unfinished.

I met Brother 3 and his wife at the airport. My stepdad picked us up from the airport. I still could not figure out how Mike got a gun. I was sitting at the end of August transitioning into September. It was only in April that all eight of us had been together for a failed attempt at a family reunion. Brother 3, his wife, and I had been at Mike's house, where he was renting a room, singing the family theme song "House of the Rising Sun." Mike got sloshed as always. I sat there babysitting his irrational slurred speech. Brother 3, like the stealth ninja he pretended to be, approached me as Mike finally broke his phone in a fit a unknown rage and fell asleep on his couch. "Mike has a gun," Brother 3 whispered. "Apparently, he took it from Sister 3, who was given it by a crazy ex-boyfriend to hide."

"What!" I whisper yelled. "He can't have a gun."

Knowing Mike had tried to kill himself before, I knew that between the evils of Mike having a gun to protect Sister 3 from herself or Sister 3 having a gun to protect the world from her, I would bet on none of the above. Not one of those scenarios was a good option, considering I knew the upbringing of both of them and knew that neither of their current lifestyle choices were conducive with being a responsible gun owner.

Brother 3 and I processed through several options that would lend being the most healthy and best choice for all involved. We concluded Brother 3 would take the gun and dispose of it properly. That was the end of the discussion for me. I left that family reunion with unintended consequences, never knowing that would be that last time I saw my brother Mike alive.

As Brother 3, his wife, and I sat in my stepdad's small extended cab on our way back to my mom's house, I repeated my thoughts on Mike's acquisition of a gun out loud. Brother 3 sat in silence. His refusal to answer me made me furious, and I repeated the question over and over and over.

"Hey!" I yelled. "Where did Mike get a gun?" knowing that Brother 3's silence revealed the gun in question was the exact same gun discussed only in April. His refusal to reply to my disbelief became evident of the answer he could not say through his tears. I looked at his wife, who sat in the scrunched back seat with me. "He feels like this is his fault," she tenderly replied.

Here, at this crossroads, I found myself in the path of two choices. Be angry at Brother 3 and blame him. Be angry at no one and blame no one but the actual person who pulled the trigger. I sat on those choices for a solid thirty minutes of that car ride. I didn't say one word to anyone, and the quiet was reciprocated.

I looked at Brother 3 and mentally sighed. My thoughts danced back and forth from personal pain he felt and the emotion that was so strong of guilt in the truck to the thoughts we both shared of the loss of our brother. I knew this was not Brother 3's fault any more than it was mine. Blame is such a knee-jerk reaction to suicide. I found that out the hard way.

Brother 3 continued to sit in silence. I don't know the thoughts pounding his skull at my previous inquiries about the gun, but as the unspoken answer of the gun never leaving Mike's apartment that night became painfully aware, I realized the grief all of us were going to feel from this was going to be so incredibly different and real. No, I did not and, still to this day, do not blame anyone for the events of Mike's suicide. I don't even know that I blame Mike.

That week was hell. I sat back and watched the circus unfold with the clarity of a drunk. Then of course, there was my mom who irritated me with every breath and uttered word. But it was my dad that I saw in some kind of different nuance of a light. This pain was new. He was new. It was not good. It was real. His oldest son. My dad cried like I had *never* seen any grown man do. He sobbed and cried and then cried and sobbed. If ever a broken heart could be seen on someone's outside, this was that moment. My dad…broke.

What does a broken man need?

My dad…broken and unable to glue any of this back together. Gold or not. It was never getting fixed.

This moment, seeing my dad's thoughts verbally leave his sober mouth would be a moment I would never be able to grasp in its entirety.

Sister 1 had gathered all of Mike's belongings and strategically set everything out in what looked like a yard sale of my brother's memories. Everything he ever owned was placed on my mom's fireplace hearth.

As I walked out to the front porch to gather my broken father and bring him inside to see if there was anything he wanted, he refused with no words, only sobs. His mental anguish was so painful to see that any pain I felt I had ever incurred by this man melted away. For I saw my dad as a man—an imperfect man with imperfect children in an imperfect world filled with perfect hope. Sitting on the porch swing with my dad felt like I was driving through an eternal school zone at 10mph. The problem as I saw it was that I was looking for the sitting police officer who monitors the zone instead of watching out for children. While no one was running over kids, I wondered where my intentions lay. I care about kids. I cared about Mike. But I was looking for the one thing that might get me in trouble and not looking for what reasons the protections were in place.

I sat down next to him on the porch swing and listened to his beating breath try to unsuccessfully capture a normal pattern. When moment after moment passed, he said with the voice of a failed parent, "Everything my son was is in that room. But he is not. What have I done?"

What could I say? I had been the recipient of his neglect and abuse. But this moment of sorrow and my father's own reality of his own mistakes were not mine to throw back in his face. My dad was facing his demons. My dad was forced to face his fears. My dad was, well, my imperfect but beautiful dad.

All in one sigh, with tears I had never before seen from a man, my dad turned his face to mine and said, "I love you, Elizabeth. I am *so* sorry. I can't fix this. I should have a long time ago. I should have said this so long ago. But I love you, and I am so sorry."

I put my arm around my dad while he learned forward in the swing, put his hairless head into his hands, and cried. For he felt the loss of his own flesh and blood at a price no parent should ever have to pay. I could not be angry at my dad for feeding us to the wolves of life.

I realized that as difficult it was to be raised with the childhood I had, it was harder for my mom and dad to have burden of being the parent of a child who died by suicide. My parents were owning their impact. I could help ease their burden by allowing them to apologize. It could not change my past, but it has changed my present outlook on life.

When I was able to see my mom, in that moment, trying to say sorry for a past she could not fix, I had to see it for the worth and value it was. At first, all I wanted to do was blame her and my dad. I wanted to yell it in their faces that Michael's suicide was their fault. But I had no words. I could not form words or identify my emotions. I only felt a mother's pain of loss. I saw my mom for the first time in the eyes I carried for myself. Her child was taken from her too.

I wondered about the people Alma the younger had offended and hurt. When Alma repented and wanted to be a better person, how difficult it must have been for them to see Alma as an imperfect person applying the atonement to his life. It must have been an incredible journey for the people Alma caused pain and sorrow to. I want to believe that someone put their arm around Alma as he cried in his hands and realized how gentle life really was.

I can't begin to describe the weight of sorrow that literally left my body when this realization came to me. I probably lost 299 pounds of mental trauma and weight! Over the next few years, I slowly started to watch my mom become personalized, instead of catastrophize.

Weirdly, life got better. I said what I needed to say. I encouraged others to say what they needed. I started to become more vocal about my needs in a much more assertive format. The effects were breathtakingly evident. I noticed my own children become happier. My husband's affect became more relaxed and trusting. My work performance improved. I desired the best in all people.

This is not to say I was not cured from all sorrow. I have my bad days. There are times I still feel worthless and useless. I am still struggling with insecurity. I battle myself and my broken past every day.

As a woman, I found (by the many women I associate with) I am not alone in my thinking. Most of the women I associate with have a story of their own. A story that has shaped them into the most beautiful people I know. But I have also learned that a bad moment is *not* the same thing as a bad day.

I am in my second marriage. I have two kids from my first marriage and three with my second. My first marriage was a disaster, but I must be honest in this claim. It was not always. There were moments of love and respect. Kindness and forgiving. Peace and compassion. Something changed, however. I stopped loving him, and he stopped loving me. And a lot of details in between.

A few years ago, after a ten-year custody battle with my ex-husband, my two older children came home to me. They had spent those young toddler years with him. I held resentment, anger, and felt defeat that only a mother who loses a child could understand. Then one day (it was night actually), it happened. They were both old enough to decide which parent they wanted to live with, and there was nothing my ex could do to stop that decision from happening. All I had to do was sit back and let it happen.

For me, a woman who lost everything, I felt as though I had gained everything back in one moment! I defined my worth by being a mother with custody. I found myself feeling embarrassed and needing to justify why I did not have custody of my two older children. I felt incorrectly judged by other women. This was realistically not the case, but my emotions of reality were so distorted by my lack of gold joints. I was trying to glue myself back together with used chewing gum. I thought having my kids back in my custody would give me back my self-worth I felt was stolen unfairly from me. I was wrong.

I don't tell my kids stories of my past to scare them into living a better life. I tell them they are enough with my stories of growth and accomplishments, that they were worth fighting for.

Bad things happen to good people. Good things happen to bad people. That is a fact. But you cannot plant a seed and eat its fruit the same day. Plant your seed of "I am enough." Nurture yourself and help yourself grow. They say the best day to plant a tree is forty years ago. The second-best day is today. Plant your seed of faith, let God nourish you and show you the worth you are, and keep repeating, "I am enough."

I was able to get a better-paying job but had to work insane hours to still make ends meet. Pete had lost his job, and I was once again the sole income to the household. My presence in the home dwindled, and having my older kids back in my care felt pointless as I never saw them, let alone anyone else in my family.

I had been working as an assistant program director for a youth in custody program designed for boys in the state of Utah's custody, who were affiliated with gangs and drugs. The boys were court ordered to our treatment program based on evidence-based practices of recovery.

For several of these youth, being in a program was safer and more stable than any home life they ever knew. One of the boys (we will call him BK) was about to graduate the program and be returned home but had self-sabotaged one too many extensions to be granted any more. The time had come, and the state would no longer allow any more excuses for him to remain in custody. BK was court ordered to return home on the following Monday.

I had been at program on Thursday night swing shift, assisting the staff with making sure BK's belongings were all inventoried and documented. Two of the other boys and I found ourselves side-tracked in the kitchen making dinner, when I noticed the presence of BK missing. I began to look around corners, calling his name, asking the other clients if they had seen him or knew where he was. I was met with empty air and a sick feeling in my gut.

I began to worry and panic. The other boys sensed my urgency to find BK and assisted in trying to locate him. I ran to the basement and looked in BK's room. Empty. I knocked on all the bathroom and shower stalls. Silence. I ran half way up the stairs and was stopped in my tracks by an unforeseen force that prompted me to go back downstairs and check the bathroom again.

As I ran back to the first bathroom, I opened up the locked shower stall to find BK hanging from a belt looped around his neck.

He could not have been there very long, but his unconsciousness was evidence to me that I did not have much time. BK was a large kid of fourteen years old, and my small frame gathered up all the strength of a mother, wrapped my arms around his waist, and reached as high as I could for the belt tied to the showerhead. I had pulled him up enough to loosen the belt from his neck. His dead weight landed on top of me and was too much for me to hold. We both fell to the floor, and I started to scream.

The other boys came running to the basement and saw BK laying on the floor, unconscious. I yelled for them to go get the other staff, which they all did. When the other staff arrived, I was able to call 911, and the ambulance showed up just in time to take BK away. He was not returned home, and his continuation into more programs and now jail were just what he wanted. Home was not a place of joy for him.

BK would often confine in me his traumatic stories of injustice in his childhood as I tried to teach him basic life skills, like saying "thank you" and "please." At the age of eleven, BK had a fourteen-year-old girlfriend who became pregnant with his child. This little girl was now two years old and often a topic of passion for BK. As a child himself, he would find it difficult to draw that connection that he needed to be a father to her as he was well aware of the lack of parental guidance in his life. But the connection never came, and BK continued to use drugs, get into assaultive fights with other clients, and self-harm. His behaviors kept him in the program for twice as long as anyone else, but it would be what he chose and wanted.

BK had a passion for music, and his favorite song is "A Team" by Ed Sheeran. Whenever BK was having a more than usual rough day, he would request I play that song for him, pause on the line, "And they scream the worst things in life come free to us…" on repeat several times, and then continue the song. This became his mantra, "The worst things in life come free to us."

BK was physically and sexually abused by his own biological father, who ended up killing himself in front of BK when BK was ten. BK's hygiene was usually an issue because of the traumatic experiences he had witnessing his father fill a plastic tub with hose water, throw his little brother in the plastic tub, and put a lid on it. BK was forced to sit on the lid of the tub while his brother nearly drowned. BK talked about the gurgling sounds of the splashing water underneath him. The sound of his brother's face pressed up to the lid with only an inch was air to spare, screaming for help and scared that he would die, still haunted him. BK disclosed this was the typical punishment for peeing the bed. When his dad would find out that the twin bed the brothers had shared had been peed in, he would drag them both outside, no matter the temperature or weather, and fill up "the tub."

One day, when a new client came into the program, as a form of boyish play, after washing his hands, the new client flicked his wet hands into BK's face. That was the worst fight I ever broke up and had to restrain BK. BK was eventually released to go into a cooldown room and proceeded to punch a hole in the two-inch thick wood-covered walls. The punch to the wall broke every bone in BK's hand. It took BK three days to calm down from having water flicked in his face. The trigger of water was something he would never be able to overcome.

When the time came for BK to return back to his mother, who was now in recovery from drugs, he was not ready. She had not been a part of his life since BK was two years old, and the speculation that she had sold BK to other men for sex in exchange for drugs did not sit well with him. He had made several comments throughout the prior two weeks that he would only leave the program dead, but no one listened or took him seriously. Until I found him hanging himself in the shower.

I lost so much weight I was down to 108 pounds. My supervisor pulled me aside and demanded I take a day off to spend with my kids.

When I told the kids I had a day off, I asked them to plan something fun. There was a local pool in the area, and with the summer heat upon us, the obvious choice became to go swimming for a few hours that afternoon. But something inside of me kept hesitating. As the kids gathered all the pool gear, tried on swimsuits, and argued over who was going to use what towel, I slowly found one task after another to delay the event. I didn't know why. I just had a strange feeling that going to the pool today would be a lot of work. I also hesitated because it was such a hot day. I knew there would be a lot of people causing the place to be packed with familiar faces I was still trying to forget from my single days of crazy living.

But my efforts were in vain, and I knew I could not prolong the inevitable day trip. Pete decided it would be a beautiful day to drive up the mountain and spend some well-needed, alone time in his favorite place on Earth. We talked about time frames and what time to plan for dinner then went our separate ways. My oldest son had an obligation somewhere with school, so the party of five headed to the local swimming pool.

As was expected, the pool was packed, and the water was inviting due to the heat blaring down on our desert land. The landscape was beautiful, and the view of the Manti Temple was astounding as I sat on the side of the pool in the kiddie section with my new baby.

The kids had all run in, dropped their belongings on a random lawn chair, and headed into the comfort of the blue water. I contemplated having my seven-year-old son put on his life jacket, but it was a couple sizes too small and had not been replaced. My oldest daughter had taken my little redheaded baby bundle of just three years old under her care while I sat in the shallow end of the pool with my new baby, watching all the excitement.

My son, age seven at the time, was tall enough to go down the slide by himself, but not a strong swimmer. When my oldest daughter was bored with the slide, she and my other daughter of three years decided the lazy river part of the pool would be more exciting. I watched back and forth at the three of them playing and enjoying their adventures while my baby sat in between my legs in the kiddie section. I had purposefully left my phone in the car so as to not be distracted by work.

As the afternoon went on, a few associates of mine found me by the side of the pool and sat down to enjoy a casual conversation in the latest of our life events.

Our conversation broke instantaneously with the sound of a loud whistle and three lifeguards running to the side of the pool, yelling for everyone to get out. I looked up at the commotion just as one of my friends asked, "Is that your son?" while I watched a young lifeguard push my son's lifeless body onto the cement side of the pool.

I took my sunglasses off to get a better look. When I realized what I did not want to see, I threw my baby into the arms of my friend and ran to the other side of the pool, where an eighteen-year-old lifeguard was performing CPR on my son. I started screaming my son's name. I don't know why. I had seen some pretty terrific events in my day, but for some reason, the sight of my seven-year-old son laying lifeless and having a bright-yellow CPR mask on his face did me in.

The other lifeguards kept asking me for information about name and age, but I was motionless and could not talk. The eighteen-year-old lifeguard stated so matter-of-factly, "I have a pulse." I looked up at him and yelled, "What the hell is going on!" He grabbed my face and said, "You are not going to be any help by panicking. I need you to calm down. Look at me. Look at me! You have to calm down." There was an older lady in the background who had been working at the front desk, explaining to 911 dispatch the situation and details I was unable to give due to my current state of shock. A pool of one hundred people of all ages, and you could have heard a pin drop. Not a person was making a sound as all eyes were on me and Wylee.

My son was blue, and his lips were purple, a shade I had never seen so fresh in my life. He was not moving, and the lifeguards continued to pump air into his lungs with a CPR mask. The sixteen-year-old girl who had pulled him from the bottom of the pool stood over us and watched. We were all on pins and needles waiting for any sign of life to arrive.

And with the last forceful push of air into my son's little lungs, he turned his head and threw up more water than I could imagine possibly could fit into one human.

My screams turned into hysterical crying. The lifeguards rolled him to his side as he continued to throw up more and more water. The ambulance had arrived and proceeded to put his body into blankets and then the gurney. He was swept away in the back of the ambulance at the same time I realized I needed to call Pete, figure out what to do with my kids, and get my crap together. I could not see my girls.

My friend immediately appeared out of nowhere and said she would take care of getting my kids home but to ride with my son to the hospital. My oldest daughter had retrieved my phone from the car and had her sister by her side. Both appeared in shock like me but capable of handling the next few moments without me as I tended to my son. I hugged my oldest daughter and ran to the ambulance that was getting ready to leave.

I called and called Pete but had little service due to him being on the mountain. When the phone finally picked up, all I got out was, "He drowned…" before the call ended.

I was still in a bathing suit standing in the cold emergency room when our family members were finally informed of the situation and came to see what was going on. My son had regained consciousness and started to lose the ugly purple color that his lips produced. His cute little pink cheeks were returning, but not his smile. He was still trying to figure out what was going on and why he was in the hospital next to his half-naked mother and fully clothed nursing staff. This was obviously not the swimming trip he had been hoping for.

Pete arrived about an hour into the hospital stay with the most heartbreaking look I have ever seen, even to this day. His only said was what he presumed to be dead. It was not until he had made it off the mountain that he learned of the ordeal. We were all alive, but the near-death drowning had tortured his soul. Pete's appearance in the emergency room was astonishing and helpless. He hugged his only biological son and namesake, who, by now, had returned to the full transparent white-skinned kid and started to cry.

He looked at me over the bed, and no words were shared. The moment was somber. We were okay physically. We would be emotionally drowned for a long time to follow.

We read in the local paper a few weeks later of a child the same age as my son who had successfully drowned in a lake just a little north of us. We wanted to feel like we were lucky, but the fact was another family was not. Gloating on luck, or God's intervention, did not seem appropriate. Every summer since our near-death drowning, I read of the inevitable young child that did drown and am instantly reminded that there will always be some that make it and some that do not.

It is all a part of a plan we were designed for. It does not mean that some are more blessed, more faithful, more loved, or more watched over. It means that faith is an action word. Faith does not mean that we believe God will intervene on our behalf for what we want, but for what He wants for us. It means, we believe in God's plan and agree to follow Him, no matter the outcome of whatever situation we find ourselves in. This might come across as easy to say, coming from someone whose child is still alive. But I have never known anything in my life to be easy. Including having faith.

Around the time BK left the program, the owners got together and decided to try and work with girls in custody, instead of boys. They asked me to be the program director, create a curriculum and program style to assist in their recovery, and hire a bunch of people for pennies on the dollar. Working with the girls was the only thing I loved about the position.

ML was eleven years old and turned twelve two days before coming to my program. She would have come a week sooner, but her mother had just passed away from cancer associated with a drug overdose, and her father was in another state in federal prison for drug distribution across state lines. ML's case manager called me and explained that ML was addicted to heroin, and after the funeral, he would drop her off to us. Christmas was just around the corner, and my already-breaking heart was trying to figure out how to help this twelve-year-old heroin addict have some Christmas magic.

IP was sixteen years old. She had just moved to Utah after her four-year-old sister was kidnapped, raped, and murdered in Arizona. Because her parents were high on meth at the time, it took them two days to even notice IP's sister missing. By the time the police found the body, IP's parents had packed everything up and moved to a homeless shelter in downtown Salt Lake City. IP was brought to our program for several drug charges after her parents forced her to sell drugs on the streets. Her Christmas morning was looking grimmer by the day.

TN was seventeen when she was found by a Salt Lake City police officer in a men's public bathroom. She was being prostituted out by a sixty-seven-year-old man in exchange for meth. She had been familiar with this practice since her mother had been prostituting her out since the age of nine. TN came to my program with a chip on her shoulder and no personal identity or sense of personal love. She trusted no one, and the only thing anyone had given her in the last seventeen years was bruises, scars, and a lifetime of self-loathing for mankind. I kept thinking there had to be something I could do to show her the world was genuinely a good place.

As I sat in my church meetings a few weeks before Christmas, I was listening to the usual announcements before one of the classes. I could *not* stop thinking about these girls and the many others out there struggling to see how joyful and beautiful the birth of Christ is and why we celebrate it so loudly every year! It was not just ML, IP, or TN I was concerned about, but it was all my girls at the program., all sharing an unfortunately traumatic past.

Many of these girls had shared with me their personal disdain for Christmas based upon the fact that they had never experienced it the way I described it. I would bounce around the building, singing or humming Christmas carols, hang lights, and put up a tree with decorations. The girls would all gather in our front room at night and stare at the lights. Some of them would comment how unreal it felt to actually have their very own tree.

Comments throughout the weeks would be how much they hated Christmas for one reason or another. IP listed her reason as that every year, some nice person or organization would feel bad for her and her siblings and bring all kinds of gifts. She said she learned not to get attached to anything, or even take it out of its box because the day after Christmas, her mom and dad would snag everything up and take it to a store to return it for money for drugs.

ML said she hated Christmas because her mom was always too sick and could never even go shopping for anything. When ML's mom was not sick, she was too high to leave the house. ML would wake up Christmas morning to find nothing under her tree.

TN had lost all hope in all mankind.

So as I sat through the announcements that beautiful Sunday, it came to me as quick as the spirit works. I needed to ask for help in giving these girls each a blanket. I raised my hand and asked if I could request sixteen blankets for the girls in my program.

I explained that the significance of a personalized blanket would mean more to these girls than any other gift that hat could possibly be given. No one could take it away and sell it for drugs. It was a promise of comfort and warmth, similar to that only given by the spirit. And it was going to be there Christmas morning, like the Savior had his swaddling blanket to hold him as he entered into this world to save us all.

My request ignited a full-blown fire! The humanitarian made personal quilts for every one of those girls. Women donated blankets for weeks! My entire living room was packed with that special magic we see over and over at Christmas time. I wrapped those blankets and carefully wrote each girl's name on the tag. I loaded those blankets in my car and delivered them under the tree at the program one day before Christmas.

As the girls gathered around that tree the night before Christmas, many cried for the first time in a really long time. I distinctly remember TN repeat the same question over and over, "Someone just *gave* these to us? But they don't even know us." This was the first time since TN had been at the program that she hugged me. We had so many blankets we were able to save some for the new girls that came in over the course of the next year. Those blankets were an answer to many prayers!

Right before IP's graduation from our program (about nine months after Christmas), she was packing up her belongings and refused to pack her blanket. That was because she took it with her everywhere. She wanted to make sure she constantly had it, and it never left her side. She wanted to make sure it did not get left behind. She told me that Christmas night how much that blanket would help her feel secure and safe.

ML cried and cried and cried. A blanket was the one thing she said she wanted because it was the one thing that would never leave her.

Those girls that Christmas morning were finally able to experience the magic of Christmas so many of us have taken for granted. It was never about, and never will be, about the price tag of the item we give a person. It will always be about the love we give and teach through Christ's example. He gave us his life so we could enjoy a little comfort once in a while. The humanitarian efforts provide that comfort we all crave. I know a bunch of drug-addicted teenage girls that will attest to that!

I shared with the women in my church the thank-yous and notes of gratitude from the girls. A couple of days later, I had several people in my community seek me out, with tears in their eyes, stating they had no idea our communities and our youth were so at risk.

We often find that if we continue to live under a rock, we will eventually hit our heads on that rock. Trauma is everyone and is not just outside the limits of your city.

I found I could connect with these kids because like so many of them, their beginnings paralleled mine. Our details were different, but our desire to belong to something bigger than ourselves was the same.

When my oldest son started out his football season his senior year, he had almost zero playing time. As a mom, I couldn't figure it out. He was so fast, he was good, and he had the biggest heart of any kid in that field. Defense was his game! But the coaches didn't play him. After the first game of the season, he felt like a failure. He only played special teams at kickoff. The weekend was rough, and by Sunday evening, I have had enough of his pouting.

I went down to his room, where he was laying in his bed and asked him what was wrong. The first thing he said was the "f" word as I like to call it. "Fine." "I'm fine," he said. I sat on his bed, and we talked about being enough.

I explained that I didn't care if he spent the entire season on the sideline, that his coaches might never see what he was worth or capable of because I knew what he was capable of. I knew he was good enough. I explained that if he was going to be on the sidelines, he was going to be the best sideline player on the team. He had no control of the coaches' decisions to play him or not. He did have control over how he acted as a team player…even on the sidelines.

I explained that as his mom, I spent several years of his childhood parenting from the sidelines waiting for God (aka "coach") to let me play. When it was finally my chance, I was ready! I jumped at the opportunity, and now that I am playing. I am trying my best.

At the next home game, we played a school called Union. A player had been injured in the game before, and now my son was in line to play. Coach put him in the front line as a defensive lineman! Let me explain, he is just a little guy! Five feet ten. *Maybe* 175. Maybe. I thought the coach was going to kill him!

But I sat back and watched a miracle unfold before my eyes! My son had seven major hits, including four sacks that game!

At the end of the game, I ran up to my son. We both embraced each other. I asked him what happened. He said he thought to himself before the game that anytime the coach put him in, he was going to hit someone like it was the last time he was ever going to play. He said he knew he could do it, just one play at a time!

By the end of the season, my son was second in the state for quarterback sacks! He played every game. He was all region, all state, and defensive lineman of the year! Not bad for a kid who didn't even play the first couple of games and went from feeling like he was nothing to feeling what it's really like to be enough!

This "sideline parenting" concept applies to all of us. Be where your feet are. Be in the moment. Be enough because all of us are enough. We may not feel like it at the moment, but it doesn't change what the reality is. Just because we doubt ourselves does not mean our Savior does. Other people may see the mistakes we make and judge us as the person who made that mistake, but we are not the entirety of the mistake.

I feel it is important to end this ongoing learning curve I am embracing on the new relationship I have with my mother. I can love her with boundaries. I have forgiven her for the mistakes she made that directly affected me. I still find myself getting frustrated with her at times, but I catch myself from falling into old unhealthy habits by reminding myself that I cannot hold grudges against others and then expect God to completely forgive me. I have to allow others room for error while still allowing myself peace.

Understanding that people make mistakes is part of the beauty of allowing ourselves the peace in moving forward with our own lives. I cannot continue to justify my own sins by using the excuses of my childhood. The notion that we behave a certain way "because of how I was raised" can only be used so far. I doubt any one of us will get into heaven "by reason of insanity." We all have full knowledge and responsibility to accept our challenges and learn from them. "Learning" means implementation.

I accept my responsibility in the execution of my wrongs or sins. Those sins had, and continued to have, nothing to do with my mother or how I was raised. I say this because I doubt Lamen and Lemuel could use the excuse of their upbringing to justify their rebellion. I also do not believe that the third of the hosts of heaven can blame their beginnings on their raising either. It also brings me to the point that God, who is the *perfect* parent, lost a third of his children. Sometimes, people just make poor choices. Sometimes, the cost of those choices is paid by unwilling or vulnerable populations, like children.

Another important part of accountability is understanding that mistakes will happen. We cannot, and will not, be protected from all the evils in the world. When Adam and Eve were in the garden of Eden, God walked daily with Adam. The perfect all-powerful, all-knowing God could not, and would not, protect Adam and Eve from the serpent. Adam and Eve had to choose for themselves to walk with God and follow His ways, or leave His presence.

As parents, we cannot, and should not, protect our children from all the evils in the world. As God did with Adam and Eve, we instruct our children on the available choices and the consequences of those choices and let them decide for themselves. Adam and Eve chose to listen to an idiot. Sometimes, we do too. Sometimes, it gets us kicked out of God's presence, but there is a way back. It is through the atonement of Jesus Christ. Good thing we have Jesus around to save us because we cannot save ourselves any more than Adam and Eve were able to get back into the garden of Eden after violating one of God's rules.

It is important to note, once again, that accountability will come. Whether in this life or the next. But it will come.

With my own mother, she has really tried to make her wrongs right with me. I appreciate that immensely. I am learning from her vulnerability and working to figure out how to implement that into the context of my own life.

Some of the best work we could do on ourselves is to give ourselves grace, allow ourselves permission to make a mistake, and realize that we can come back from that mistake. If you complain about life, it's because you are only thinking of yourself. The thinking error is believing that once we have made a mistake, there is no coming back.

We have become a culture of complainers. We are not willing to work unless the carrot is dangling in front of us. What happened to working because working was good for us. We all jumped on bandwagons of diets and the latest type of exercise but look for the easiest and least resistant way to confront our inside and emotional health if it takes work! Put in that work! Stop complaining and start working.

There is always a comeback.

This brings me to where I am today.

I am back working with the state of Utah as a CPS investigator. But this time, I am employed as a related party investigator. I investigate the investigators, the conflicts of interest, the high-profile cases, and the cases that DCFS cannot. I came back because the children in this state need me, and I will not let them down. I am once again working with kids and their trauma, investigating abuse and finding my way through the red tape.

It feels different this time. It feels better and more fulfilling. The great thing about staying with a job you love in a career that finds new challenges and is always changing is that I am never bored. And I see the payoff.

I have never cried in an interview with a child. Now, honestly, I've come close, but I have never actually cried in an interview before *until...*

I received a case for PF. He was transitioning from a girl to a boy. I don't want to get into politics or personal religious views about this topic. For this line of work, all that is irrelevant. Because abuse has no boundaries, there is no room for bias when it comes to the safety of children.

PF was thirteen years old and had been in foster care with his brother since the age of five. PF had been locked in a closet for most of his life, only to be let out and raped by one of his mother's clients. PF used the same litter box with the family cat in a locked closet and ate the scraps of whatever food was found on the floors of the home when his mother forgot to lock him back up.

One day, his mom left, and her body was found three states away, naked and brutally beaten to death. PF and his brother were discovered by a caring neighbor, who kept hearing the sounds of the crying cats and became concerned. After being taken into custody, PF and his brother bounced from home to home to home.

Neglect can manifest itself in the worst ways and mock diagnoses of ADHD, learning disabilities, and reactive attachment disorder. PF and his brother were so difficult to handle that at several points, they were split up into different homes and then placed back together, and then split up again. The shelters were on a first-name basis with the two children, and it was extremely unusual for them to be in a home for longer than one month at a time.

Not only were the foster homes quick to turn the two children out, but the caseworkers also switched so quickly. Reading the history of PF made one worker just quit, citing this was not the job they had signed up for. PF and his brother had no idea who was even making decisions for them anymore.

And then I got the case. PF had claimed he had been in an emotionally abusive foster home, and I was assigned to investigate.

I met PF at fourteenth school he had been enrolled in over the last three years. I reviewed my job title, responsibilities, and why I was there to talk to him. I called him the name he requested out of respect for what he wanted to identify as, not his legal gender or name.

Despite my personal beliefs, I had learned early on in this job that I needed to meet people where they were, not where I wanted them to be or what my personal belief system was. PF was entitled to that dignity and respect, and I was not going to be the one to stand in his way. I also learned I am allowed to have and hold strong to my personal beliefs as long as they do not interfere with my work. I am allowed to believe in my faith and respect others for who they are.

Upon our introductions, I did ask for the clarification on his legal name (had to make sure I had the right kid). He quickly told me that he believed girls are the ones abused, not boys. So he wanted to be a boy so people would stop abusing him.

The tears started to weld up in my eyes, but I caught them in time. We may never understand why someone would live a different lifestyle than what we would choose, but I had learned that I do not have to understand. I just have to listen. I had to take all the passion I had for the safety of children and turn it into compassion for their journey. Saying what I believe to be right and correcting all the world's wrongs will not stop the wrongs from happening.

It may be truthful, but is it helpful?

And with that, I just sat and listened to PF's story. Whatever he wanted to say, I wanted to listen. I could not fix it, or take away the pain, but I could be a compassionate listener.

By the end of the interview and gathering of evidence, I thanked PF for talking to me. I asked PF if he had any questions for me. There was an eerie pause while PF lowered his head and stared at his old beat-up converse shoes, covered in personal ink drawings and writings.

PF never looked up at me while he took a big sigh and shared that he always wondered what it would have been like to eat a meal at a dinner table with two parents asking him questions about his day, engaging in conversations with them about life and the world. PF stated he wished the world would be innocent again for him and that he could go back to a time when his emotional needs were met, not just his physical needs. He described the loss of both, and that overcompensating with the giving of one need does not overflow into something else.

I kept listening and listening, and as the interview closed in around the last school hour, he stood up to leave. I thanked PF for talking to me and stood up with him. There was a small desk between us in the corner of the supply room the school secretary had stuck us in. As PF reached for the door to leave, he turned to me and asked, "Can I have a hug? It's been so long since anyone has given me a hug, and I can't remember the last time I hugged someone."

Generally, I make it a strict practice not to hug or touch clients. I mean, duh! But with this request, I did not even pause. As I said, "Absolutely," and hugged PF like he was my own son, it felt like I was sending him off to school for the day. I could no longer hold back the tears. He cried as well and said thank you and left for class like it was another normal day.

A few years ago, I had a conversation with a good friend of mine that is a therapist for children. She suggested to me that when a client asks her for a hug, she will always embrace the opportunity. There is evidence to suggest the importance of the "gentle touch theory" and the implications for good that it can have on children. My friend stated that whenever she is hugged by a client, she never ends the hug first. She suggested that you may never know how life-saving that hug could be.

I have implemented that very principle into interactions with my own children. I never break the hug first. And I did not do it with PF. I just let PF hug me for as long as he needed. It should be noted that it was only a few seconds, but it was a few seconds of comfort that helped him know his voice was heard, and I would be taking action against his predator.

After receiving and investigating hundreds of cases, my desire to end child abuse grows stronger by the day. It is terrible work that should not even have to be done. It is 2024, and the world is full of resources and opportunities to better the lives of children and their families. Why is abuse still alive and well? Are you kidding me?

I can't sleep at night. I eat in the car between visits and interviews. I overprotect my children. I overreact to the simplest crisis. I crave being drunk everyday (but I don't.) I yell and scream profanity at my computer screen while typing case notes. And I go to church every Sunday because I know that at least there, I can find the love of Jesus. I need more Jesus in my life.

My message is for every caseworker, judge, prosecutor, law enforcement officer, guardian ad litem, and parent. If I can do this, you can do this! You *have* to do this. It's time we fight together for the children and not the predator. There should be no more excuses. Use your position to better the lives of our little ones. Don't give up on your voice. Remember, we all have a story, and the children today will tell your story as they have mine.

I am here and alive. I am okay. I am breathing and embraced. Sometimes I feel sad because of the inactions of others. Sometimes I feel happy by the actions of others. I know I am loved, and I am learning to understand what knowing love really means. I can be happy and sad, feel accomplished and a failure all in one day. But I will get through it because I know, right now, in *this* moment, I am the fighter for every unhugged, starving, abused, and neglected child! I am the child's champion. I am Elizabeth!

ABOUT THE AUTHOR

ELIZABETH ALLRED GRADUATED WITH A bachelor's degree in sociology in 2003, a master's degree in psychology in 2013, and obtained her Social Service Worker license all while either being nine months pregnant, or holding her newborn baby in her arms. Elizabeth's passion for child welfare comes from a place of lived experiences as the oldest of eight children in a dysfunctional family. In 2005, Elizabeth was excommunicated from the Church of Jesus Christ of Latter-Day Saints, and in 2012, her brother Michael shot and killed himself, leaving Elizabeth forced to come to terms with the realities of her buried past.

Elizabeth started out with the Division of Child and Family Services in 2004, left after a terrible divorce, remarriage, and desire to see the world with nontraumatic eyes. However, after being a dorm parent at an international boarding school, a cheerleading coach, a program director for youth in custody for boys with behavioral and gang-related charges and girls with substance use disorders, Elizabeth found herself back with the state of Utah as child abuse investigator. With over twenty years' experience, Elizabeth has been on a mission to protect children with an unapologetic voice for their safety.

Today, Elizabeth is the proud mother of five beautiful children. She has been rebaptized into her faith, married to the love of her life, and is proudly putting down roots in a small town tucked under the beautiful Horseshoe Mountain.